High-Country Lark

High Country Lark

An invitation to Paradise

NEVILLE PEAT

Longacre Press

The writing of this book was completed with the support of the Creative New Zealand Michael King Writers' Fellowship 2007.

Published 2008 by Longacre Press
30 Moray Place, Dunedin

ISBN 978 1 877460 14 2

A catalogue for this book is available from
the National Library of New Zealand.

Design by Christine Buess and Katy Yiakmis
All photographs by Neville Peat unless otherwise stated
Map by Allan Kynaston
Printed by Printlink, Wellington

www.longacre.co.nz

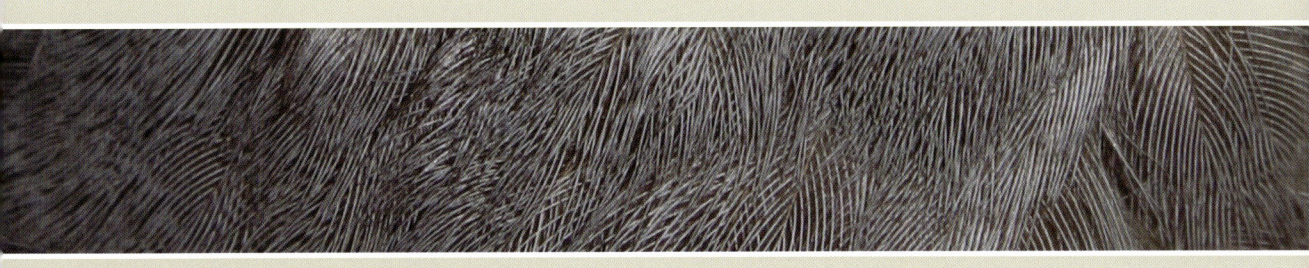

Contents

The Scene

Mountains nuzzle mountains
White-bearded rock-fronted
In perpetual drizzle.

Rivers swell and twist
Like a torturer's fist
Where the maidenhair
Falls of the waterfall
Sail through the air.

The mountains send below
Their cold tribute of snow
And the birch makes brown
The rivulets running down.

Rock, air and water meet
Where crags debate
The dividing cloud.

In the dominion of the thorn
The delicate cloud is born,
And golden nuggets bloom
In the womb of the storm.

Denis Glover, from
Arawata Bill: A Sequence of Poems, 1953

Sugarloaf Stream swing bridge.

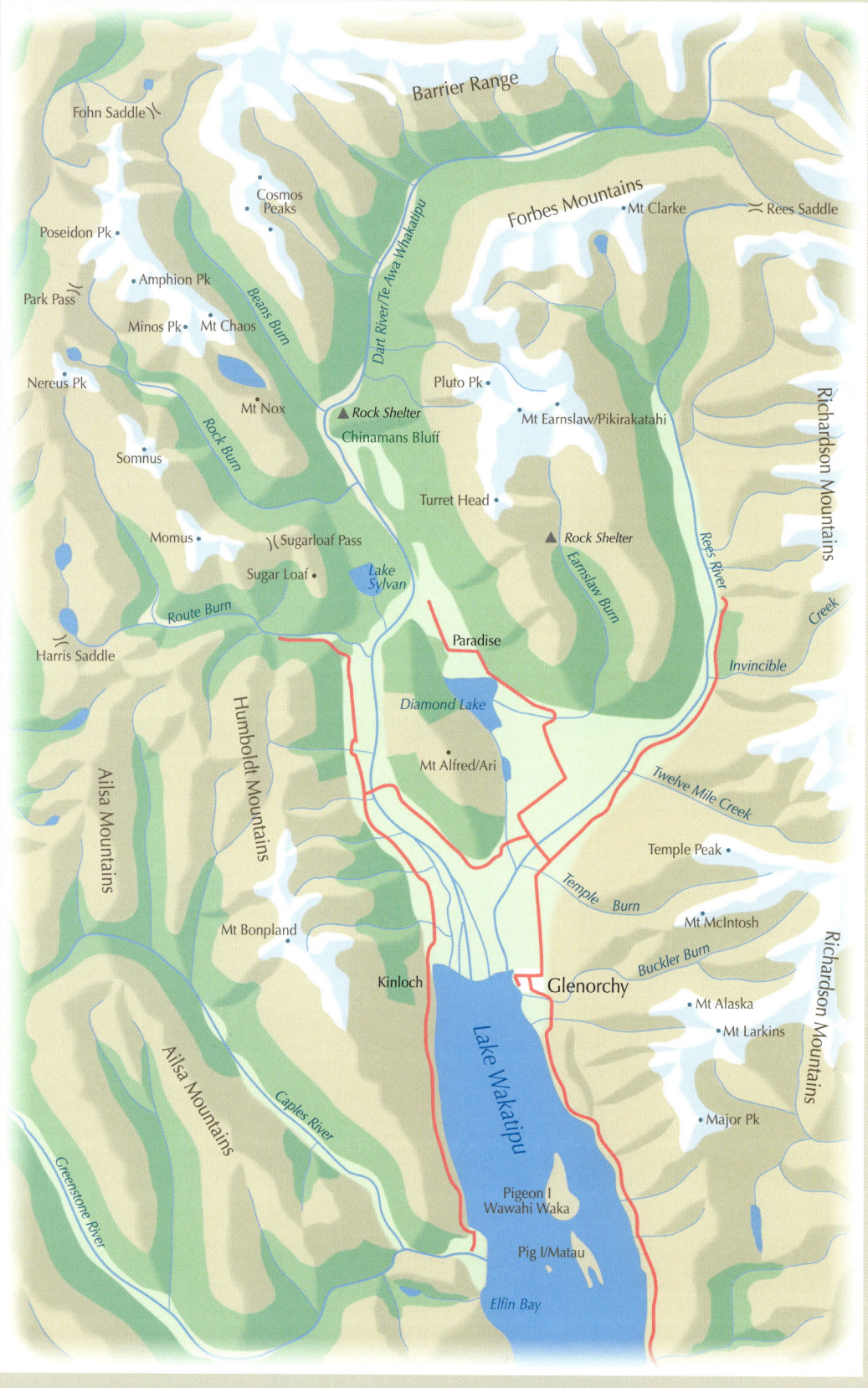

An Invitation

The invitation arrived in the post on a day somewhere between spring and summer. It was rock-solid. Inside the A5 bubble bag was a flat piece of stone, saucer thin. From the shade of grey, the smoothness of the surfaces and the brittle edges, I guessed it might be schist, the country rock of inland Otago. Scratched on one side, in pencil, were the words:

Sugarloaf Pass.
Solstice 21/12, Noon.
Deo Volente.
Lark

The cryptic message, more like a summons, was from a high-country acquaintance of mine, the Lark. The Glenorchy postmark told me the rendezvous location. Sugarloaf Pass was off the Routeburn Track in the mountains north of Glenorchy. I looked for a return address. There wasn't one. That didn't surprise me. I knew the Lark to be a free and independent traveller. He practically coined the term.

I'd last seen him at Taieri Mouth in the late 1990s, when I was looking out for the New Zealand sea lions on the beach there, and he turned up with a white-water kayak in the hope of gambolling in the surf with one of the sea lions. In earlier years I encountered him in the handsomely wide Strath Taieri valley, through which the Taieri River runs. At the time I was researching my ancestral roots there. The Peats farmed the Strath Taieri district from the 1870s, and the Aysons (my mother's side) arrived in the valley around the turn of the century. The Lark, no relation of mine at all, worked on the district's sheep farms — an itinerant shepherd and rouseabout. He knew a lot about the nature of the place, its plant and bird life, and especially its falcons. In spare moments — and there were a fair few of those — he would go hang-gliding, with or without his trusty sheepdog, Rocky. In the right place (usually the skyline of Taieri Ridge, above the dun landscape of schist tors and tussock grasses), and at the right time (when thermals allowed a glider to soar), he could be joined in the air by a young falcon he'd rescued as a chick. He had a few yarns in him, the Lark.

Now, seemingly, he had more for me. The invitation to meet him in a wild spot in the high country included the phrase 'Deo Volente' (Latin for 'God willing'). DV, for short. The Lark used to call my ageing Commer camper van Dee Vee after the letters on the number plate, DV4332. He saw in the letters a phrase his father brought home from war service in Italy.

But what was the Lark doing in the mountains and valleys way out west? He had to be well into his sixties by now. I couldn't imagine his retirement. I reached for an atlas. It placed Sugarloaf Pass at 1,154 metres and accessible from near the start of the Routeburn Track, a popular alpine tramping experience that crossed the Main Divide. The Lark had always been fit. In the Strath Taieri he could spend hours chasing hoggets down from the tops for crutching. He could blade shear sheep all day. Mustering rangeland country on foot, he seemed able to flow up hills — or used to, anyway.

What did I know of the Glenorchy area, the Head of Lake Wakatipu? Battalions of trampers, and I have been among them at times, pass through this landscape every summer. Routeburn. Rees-Dart. Greenstone-Caples. These are celebrated names for any outdoors enthusiast. Most people stick to the tracks. The Lark, I reckon, would want to avoid the beaten ones.

For motorists the Head of the Lake is a cul-de-sac, road's end. It is also the western limit of farming in Otago. Its steep mountains, tumbling rivers, moss-bedecked beech forest, and snow and ice in high places speak of a mountain fastness and wilderness dramatically arrayed — 'Middle Earth'. Some scenes in *The Lord of the Rings* movie series were filmed here. I knew, too, the district had a place called Paradise; a road sign says so. Less obvious are the characters who've called the Head of the Lake home over the years, from the refined to the rough-and-ready. Some have become legends. Bill O'Leary for one — Arawata Bill, frontiersman.

The Head of the Lake is still a frontier, the edge of Mount Aspiring National Park. It ought to be a haven for wildlife. For a number of native birds, though, life is a struggle. Mohua (yellowhead), South Island robin, kaka, kea and rock wren inhabit this frontier — but only tenuously. Introduced predators give them a hard time. Then there is the saga of the South Island kōkako, the so-called orange-wattled crow, declared extinct by the Department of Conservation in 2007. There have been unconfirmed sightings, or reports of kōkako-like calls, in valleys bordering the Head of the Lake as recently as the mid-1990s. Elsewhere in the South Island, intermittent reports continue to come in — even as I write this story — from people claiming to have glimpsed or heard kōkako in remote places. I am intrigued. I need to know more. This invitation from the Lark is timely.

Heaven's Gate, Paradise. The figure is thought to be Joseph Fenn.

HOCKEN COLLECTIONS UARE TAOKA O-HĀKENA SO7-274A-E483/26

CHAPTER 1

Accessing Paradise

Devon cream and sunny lakes
Snowy Peaks and currant cakes
Strawberries and moonlight walks
Home made wine and pleasant talks

Feed on the glories of the Dart
Sandwiches and Rhubarb tart

An entry in the Paradise House Visitors' Book in the 1890s.

At Bennett's Bluff, 200 metres above Lake Wakatipu and about halfway along the Queenstown-Glenorchy road, you can pull off the road and inspect a map highlighting the landmarks. On a clear afternoon, with the view mesmerising and the sun lowering in front of you, pulling up is advisable. It's a long way down if you make a mistake trying to take in the views while driving. In the distance is Paradise. You can't quite see it but you know it is somewhere in the press of snowy mountains beyond the lake and its dark islands. This is the area generally dubbed the Head of the Lake. A tarseal snake coaxes the eye along the foot of the Richardson Mountains. In the foreground is Meiklejohns Bay, which, on a balmy December afternoon, looks like a Club Med setting. Not that you need to see another resort area. Queenstown is quite enough, a town that markets scenery and mainlines adrenalin. Bumper-to-bumper traffic at peak times, clusters of construction cranes and a blur of advertising signs together mark the frantic face and pace of an international tourist destination. You crawl on through, feeling relief as a road sign announces the exit to Glenorchy.

At Bennett's Bluff, take a break, take your bearings, let the dramatic skyline own your appetite for new horizons. In the late 1870s, the Melbourne-based Austrian artist Eugène von Guérard did just that, though seemingly from a bit farther up the lake and from a lower vantage point. He recorded the scene in an oil painting about the size of a door sideways, titled 'Lake Wakatipu with Mount Earnslaw, Middle Island, New Zealand'. I saw it when an exhibition celebrating 200 years of New Zealand landscape painting toured the country. It captures the vivid morning light, the haughty twin peaks of Mount Earnslaw/ Pikirakatahi and their white pinafore, the Earnslaw glacier; arrowheaded Mt Alfred as a centrepiece; Sugarloaf a foothill out to the left; and seductive valleys everywhere, with the whole peaked panorama reflected on a turquoise lake. Never mind the overly-steepened mountains, an art style of the era, nature here appears all-powerful, even God-ordained. Solitude abounds amid the grandeur. But see what the artist has also caught: a vessel under sail, crossing the lake and somehow finding a breeze. It resembles a Māori waka of ocean-going size — a noble invention, perhaps added for scale.

Von Guérard, who worked out of the National Gallery of Victoria in Melbourne, produced the painting from sketches he made during his New Zealand visit. He would have been in his mid-sixties then. How did he reach his vantage point? By boat, or by walking or riding the rough bridle track from Queenstown? He was ninety years too early to travel by a proper road, and about ten years too early to appreciate guest-house hospitality at Glenorchy.

Except for the sailboat, his expansive view of the Head of the Lake contains no sign of human activity. Twenty years after von Guérard's tour, in 1898, the Head of the Lake was featured in an issue of postage stamps — recognition of the area's scenic power and increasing prominence. These stamps were New Zealand's very first pictorial issue. Curiously, the artist placed a sailboat on the lake, just as von Guérard had done. The picture even replicated von Guérard's grove of cabbage trees in the foreground. The 'Mt. Earnslaw' scene, less panoramic than von Guérard's, adorned the 2½d stamp. The scene was accurate enough but the spelling of the location as 'Lake Wakitipu' did cause a stir. The stamps were swiftly reprinted.

In those days, the lake's name was likely to be abbreviated to 'Wakatip', and you still hear the lake called that. Here's what the nineteenth-century English novelist, Anthony Trollope, wrote in 1872: 'I do not know that lake scenery can be finer than that of the upper ten miles of Wakatip.' The 'tip' bit is a contraction of 'tipua', the Māori word for something devilish, which hints at a Māori legend involving a giant ogre named Matau, who lived by himself in the hills. The story tells of his kidnapping a beautiful maiden and his subsequent demise at the hands of her rescuer, who set fire to the ogre as he slumbered through a spell of hot north-west föhn winds typical of the area. The fire was so intense it burnt a deep trench in the landscape, which is why the lake is a giant zig-zag, with the northern reach his upper body, the middle reach his thighs with Queenstown at the kneecap, and the southern part his lower legs. His heart survived cremation, though, and still beats at the bottom of the lake, at a prodigious depth, below sea level, causing lake levels to rhythmically rise and fall.

Science explains this phenomenon as a 'seiche', from a Swiss term that infers sinking. Apparently Switzerland's Lake Geneva is similarly affected. Lake Wakatipu's mini-tides, ranging up to twenty-five centimetres in height and spaced at five to fifty-minute intervals, are caused by variations in atmospheric pressure, winds and water temperatures. They interact in a baffling way. Hydrologists and mathematicians resort to tongue-tying terminology to try to explain it. The lake's distinctive shape is not easily explained by science, either. A fault line today cuts across the middle of it, about where the backside of the prostrate ogre might have lain. One theory is that the enormous glacier that gouged the bed was simply following drainage channels in terrain much older than the existing mountains.

Enough of the uncertainty. Here are some facts: Lake Wakatipu is New Zealand's longest lake, at seventy-seven kilometres, and the country's third

A Romantic panorama — the Eugène von Guérard painting of Lake Wakatipu, looking towards the Head of the Lake.

Rees River bridge.

largest after Taupo and Te Anau. It first appeared on maps of southern New Zealand in the 1840s (a decade before any Europeans had clapped eyes on the lake, let alone explored its upper reaches) thanks to Māori informants who recounted the oral maps of inland trails.

For Māori travellers of old, the Head of the Lake was a richly rewarding source of a distinctive kind of pounamu or greenstone — and that's another story. However you view the Head of the Lake today, the reality is inescapable. It's both an impressive destination and a road-block. The most distant mountains you see from Bennett's Bluff guard the Main Divide, and there is no way through for an overlander except on foot.

Beyond Bennett's Bluff, therefore, expect to feel a heightened sense of seclusion. You turned a significant corner a while back that opened up the northern arm of the lake, and now Earnslaw country is drawing you in:

Earnslaw, Eagle's Hill in the old Scots tongue. You pass a cluster of islands — first, Pig Island/Matau, low-lying and scrubby, then Pigeon Island/Wāwāhi Waka, larger and hillier, where, all too often in the past, visitors' fires have wiped out tracts of red beech, totara and matai and made life more difficult for the native pigeon, called kūkūpa in the south. These islands, together with tiny Tree Island on the far side of Matau, faced an uncertain future through the ice ages for they lay in the path of the massive Wakatipu Glacier, half a kilometre deep at this point. Its grinding, chiselling power created Pigeon Island's rounded hillocks.

Farther on, as if to reassure a visitor of connections with the outside world, Glenorchy airfield — small planes only — looms up on the left on a terrace. The town is not in sight yet, but a bronze plaque mounted on a rock commemorates the completion of the tarsealing of the Queenstown-Glenorchy road in 1997. Before then, motoring was a hazardous experience of billowing dust, flying stones and passing bays in places where the road was hair-raisingly narrow.

Coming off the airfield's terrace you cross the Buckler Burn, deeply entrenched in a narrow, sunless gorge, then the road swings left, straightens up and gently descends along the edge of the Buckler Burn's shingle fan. Glenorchy is a corner away.

Meanwhile, something is happening to the Humboldt Mountains that form the far side of the lake. Since you passed the islands, this mountain chain has steadily grown in stature in anticipation of its destiny at the Main Divide, meeting point of the east-west watershed. Okay, it's an illusion but for a few moments the Humboldts do appear to be rising before your eyes, and they are suddenly close and wildly forbidding, forest-clad more than half the way to their ragged crest.

'Welcome to Glenorchy,' says a sign at the outskirts of town. 'Gateway to Paradise.'

There are Pūkeko striding across the streets of Glenorchy, looking like they own the place, when I drive in from the Pacific coast in Christmas week, and there are parakeets sprinting across the air space above the village, fearing perhaps an attack by a falcon stooping to conquer. I have heard there are falcons camped in the pine trees on the edge of Glenorchy, and when people come too close to where they're nesting, they will fly fast and furiously

Uniform blue — but for Glenorchy's mountain backdrop, lake would meet sky.

at them. A visitor had a pair of sunglasses perched on her forehead whipped right off her head. How wild is that?

Two teenagers are riding horses on the grass verges in town. There are no formed footpaths here. Come to think of it, there are horses all over the place, grazing paddocks and hot-wired rectangles marked out for subdivision — a scene set to tempt a townie. Glenorchy, population about 200 (300 if you include the outlying runholder families, rural lifestylers and the little settlements of Paradise and Kinloch), is low-profile and laid-back. It is so close to the Head of the Lake that it occupies a river delta at the junction of the lake and feeder rivers. There is the Rees River and a set of lagoons on one side, kept at bay by flood banks, and a smaller mountain torrent, the Buckler Burn, on the other. The town is a flat and spacious grid of streets without street numbers. If you reside here, you are likely to know where most folk live.

And they tend to live in houses painted muted colours: brown, beige, Railways red and various shades of green — colours straight out of a red beech forest. The houses are typically clad in weatherboard timber or corrugated iron, sometimes a combination of the two. Glenorchy is not big on trophy homes — not yet anyway. I've noticed subdivision names like Wildburn and Pigeon Place, yet to be fully developed, on a drive around the village. Perhaps the present character is set to change.

There is definitely a new object at the town's main intersection — new since I was last here — that smacks of big-town status. A roundabout. Queenstown is a parade ground for them. But Glenorchy's sole roundabout, installed to direct visitors safely towards the Routeburn Track, it seems, is half the diameter and half the height of the Queenstown models. The speed humps on the main street are low-rise, too. They look like flat stones from the local landscape.

Although the summer solstice sun is still high, the afternoon is wearing on. I fancy a drink and a bite to eat in a pub. Glenorchy has been a pub town for 120 years. Three hotels launched the town's reputation for hospitality in the late 1880s. There are two today. Hotels and lodges are still downtown Glenorchy's largest buildings, but take note: the tallest built things in town are the rugby goal-posts in the Recreation Ground. That piece of information I get from the barman as I order a beer.

'See you've got a roundabout now.'

'That's for visitors,' says the barman. 'Locals don't take much notice. Drive over the top of it. It's designed for dinky little rental cars. Turning's too blinken tight for a decent four-wheel drive. Where you off to?'

'Paradise.'

'Could do worse.'

And with that ambiguous statement my conversation with the barman concludes. He has more glasses to fill.

I retreat to a bar stool and high table, the kind that used to have a sunken, water-filled jam jar in the middle for receiving cigarette butts. In one corner the racing channel is blaring on television and it's not even Saturday. No one is watching. Australian horse racing, I guess. There are two communities present: visitors and locals. Lined up at the bar with a shot glass in front of each of them are three women who look like they might be having a gap year Down Under. They speak an enlivened sort of English with European accents. Their banter suggests they are city people who've recently survived a challenge in the wilds — tramping, horse-trekking or jet-boating, perhaps all three. The wedges of lemon and little saucer of salt indicate tequila is their tipple. The next round goes down the hatch with the drinkers' eyes squinting from the squeeze of lemon.

'Cheers! I love you!' one of the women says to a companion.

An entirely different kind of socialising is going on in another part of the bar, around high tables pulled together. They're local men, talking rough in a huddle that says they are well used to each other's company. Dressed for outdoors work, these Southern Men are drinking — what else? — Speight's three-star, gold-medal beer out of large brown bottles, as their fathers might have done, and their grandfathers, too.

I leave town for Paradise, fed and watered, before the sun goes down behind the Humboldt Mountains. Fluffy slow-moving scraps of cumulus over Bold Peak, happy-go-lucky clouds, promise fine weather tomorrow for the Sugarloaf Pass experience. Trust the Lark to sort that out.

For an idea of weather coming up, Head of the Lake people tend to look to the Fiordland forecast. Their area lies in the transition zone between awesomely wet Fiordland/South Westland and semi-arid Central Otago. The Main Divide

Paradise named

Paradise shelducks inhabit the Diamond Lake shoreline and paddocks in the vicinity, and it's been suggested this is how the area got its name. But then, 'parries' are common throughout the Head of the Lake and no more distinctive around Diamond Lake than anywhere else. Thankfully, there is another, more colourful story about the naming. Alfred Duncan, pioneer shepherd, wrote of a chance meeting with a young Māori woman called Ruahine, the daughter of a Māori chief, at Diamond Lake in the early 1860s. She had to leave in haste, possibly as a result of invasion by another tribe. 'My heart is with you,' she wrote in a farewell note to Duncan, 'and when I die … my spirit will return to our paradise.' Duncan wrote a journal of his time at the Head of the Lake, and had his story published. Later he would write with less certainty about a romance with a Māori maiden, suggesting it might have been a dream. Still, Paradise inspired a few romantic novels, and Duncan's story, fiction or not, is a worthy precursor.

The area around Diamond Lake was soon mapped as Paradise. By the time Joseph Fenn arrived to buy up land, twenty years after Duncan, he was listed as 'Farmer of Paradise' on the titles. Incidentally, Duncan's boss, the Rees Valley runholder and first settler of Queenstown, William Gilbert Rees, named Diamond Lake, saying it looked 'like a diamond set in emeralds'.

In keeping with the mythical nature of the names Paradise and Arcadia, Biblical terms abound in the area. Heaven's Gate used to stop horse-and-buggy traffic on the forest-clad road beside Diamond Lake, and not far away was a tapered, coffin-shaped rock called Peter's Tomb, complete with a natural headstone. The River Jordan is the creek crossing the road just before Arcadia comes into view. The Garden of Eden is a small woodland clearing close to Paradise House. On the hill above it are the Rock of Ages — sheer-sided and the size of a two-storey house — and Adam's Armchair, a seat on the stump of a giant wind-thrown red beech tree, with curving buttresses for arms.

Arcadia house.

mountains create a rainshadow. It might be bucketing down for hours at the Main Divide and the valley heads facing Glenorchy, yet blowing dust off the Dart River delta all day. So fine is the dust, Glenorchy people say it gets into their houses even with all windows and doors shut.

I'm booked into Paradise for the night. It's a good twenty minutes' drive due north of Glenorchy, deeper into the mountains, closer to the daddy of them all, Earnslaw. I cross the concrete bridge over the Rees River, still on tarseal. The Rees and Dart/Te Awa Whakatipu Rivers, the lake's major tributaries, pour water into adjacent deltas and are slowly pushing the Head of the Lake southwards as floods transport gravel en masse out of their catchments. To keep Routeburn Track patrons happy, not to mention safer, the tarseal extends all the way to the Dart Bridge these days. The road network splits three ways. Left for the Dart and Routeburn, right for the Rees, and straight up the middle for Paradise. It's a no-exit outcome whichever way you go, and the Paradise road, beyond the little settlement, turns into a rutted farm track and eventually a trampers' track.

The approaches to Paradise are something out of Romantic art. Picture the

Mementoes: a postcard-size photograph of young Joseph Fenn alongside his Cambridge rowing medal, laid on the endpapers of an old Arcadia guest book.

rushing glacier-fed waters of the Earnslaw Burn emerging from a forested gorge, Diamond Lake glittering at the foot of Mt Alfred, and a red beech forest of enchanting character with the narrow gravel road zig-zagging around trees and a small section of lake shore. Over a stony ford in a creek, more sheep and cattle graze. Now the Arcadia homestead demands your attention, and not for the first time you wonder how the area came to be so delectably named.

Arcadia was an idyllic land of ancient Greece where mountains, forests and cultivated fields were happily juxtaposed, where shepherds tended sheep and brindle cattle, and nymphs inhabited shady groves. Arcadia Station, near the Head of Lake Wakatipu, is, well, with the exception of the nymphs maybe, a similar sort of environment. Brindle cattle graze contentedly on well-watered pastures bordered by national park forest and neck-stretching peaks. The Simmental cattle, a Swiss breed with cream patches on cuddly reddish-brown coats, belong to Arcadia Station. But it is not the cattle that cause travellers on the Paradise road to pull over; it is the two-storey homestead, which occupies a sylvan setting a couple of hundred metres off the road. It has 'stately home' and 'history' written all over it. Conical turrets, balconies and tall windows underscore its elegance. This is the home of Jim Veint and his partner, Ros Angelo, who own Arcadia Station and its renowned Simmentals. The farm comprises 276 hectares of freehold land stretching north of Diamond Lake to meet the Dart River.

The founder of Arcadia Station, Joseph Cyprian Fenn, named the place. A young Englishman of means, Fenn settled here in 1881, initially acquiring 800 acres to run cattle, and building a cottage for himself above the road, at the edge of the beech forest. Fenn was in his mid-twenties, a graduate of Cambridge University, a classics scholar and champion oarsman. He was not only alone, he was reclusive, and Glenorchy gossip cast long shadows. It was said he came to New Zealand because he'd been thwarted in love — his father had stolen his fiancée. Here was a legend in the making.

Presumably hurt and embarrassed, Fenn looked around for a place to live as far away from friends and family as he could get. He chose to make his home in a country at the ends of the earth from Europe, and once there, ensconced himself in one of its most isolated places. He ended up with 1,314 acres of freehold land. Imagine the reaction of the locals … Could this be a 'remittance man' with a significant inheritance come amongst us? And why was he so keen on seclusion? It was said he never opened the many letters that arrived for him from England.

In 1906–07, Fenn had the Arcadia Guest House built in red beech timber from the area, with little expense spared. It contained a smoking room and library, sitting and dining rooms, a handsome staircase to the upper storey where most of the thirteen bedrooms were located, tiled bathrooms, fireplaces with metal backs decorated with cherubs at work, ornate oriental wallpaper and Japanese friezes. An annexe built four years later expanded the accommodation.

Fenn, however, opted to stay in his cottage, about 500 metres away. He employed managers to run the guest house. Paradise House, just down the road, was also in the business of offering hospitality to visitors from afar; indeed, was better known than Arcadia, though smaller. The Aitken family ran it. David Aitken was a tall Scots goldminer who had worked in the Shotover fields before moving to Paradise. Fenn is said to have taken a shine to his daughter, Isabella,

Paradise House today.

also known as Poppy. But she had other ideas. The spurned suitor, according to rumour, built the mansion at Arcadia to show Poppy what she had missed out on.

Fenn left scant written record of his endeavours at Arcadia, and all that remains of his cottage is a broken-down chimney. But there are mementoes, handed on to the Veints from the previous owners. The most striking item is a medal won by Fenn in 1877 as a member of the Cambridge rowing eight in the traditional river race against Oxford University. There was a dead heat that year. A collar-and-tie portrait of Fenn, who is wearing a sports jacket and what looks like a boating cap, reveals a smooth-faced, sharp-eyed young man with sensitive lips — a face full of promise, innocent of the love-tortured times ahead. Also in the Veints' keeping is a flyer advertising the guest house ('9s per day, 45s per week … conveyance meets every steamer at Glenorchy … Diamond Lake trout a speciality'), and a three-handled, glass-bottomed pewter tankard, with the words, 'Champion of the Cam', engraved on it. Also engraved are the names of rivers rowed. I try to imagine Fenn packing it in his suitcase or valise with his other mementoes of a heartbreaking home. A previous owner of

Arcadia carried fence staples around in it.

The Veints themselves have added lustre to the Arcadia story. A Simmental cattle breeder of national standing, Jim Veint won the Sydney Royal Show Supreme Award two years running with his stud animals — the cattle-breeding equivalent of winning the Melbourne Cup. His father, Lloyd, became the third owner of Arcadia in 1951 following four years on the Paradise property. Lloyd was manpowered into scheelite mining at Glenorchy during the war then turned to working the land. At the time, Arcadia leased Crown land a long way up the Dart River, including all the flats on the true left side north of Dan's Paddock. Jim, his only son, has owned the property fully since 1978. He grew up here, 'the luckiest kid on earth'.

The Veints have occupied Arcadia longer than Joseph Fenn but Fenn's name will forever hover enigmatically over the farm and fetching homestead.

It is amusing to compare Fenn with another solitary nineteenth-century character, the American writer, philosopher and naturalist Henry David Thoreau. Thoreau, a Harvard graduate, withdrew from society (Concord, Massachusetts) and for a while, in the 1840s, lived in a simple hut by Walden Pond, a small wooded lake. He read Greek and Latin. He never married. But unlike Fenn, Thoreau wrote plenty about nature and the human condition. Head of the Lake history is the poorer for what Fenn never wrote down.

Paradise is another story, albeit intertwined with Arcadia's, and I am about to be introduced to it by Geoff and Grace Ockwell, managers of the property. Geoff, a Master's student in physical education at the University of Otago, is exploring local history and the way people relate to the land. He is clearly fascinated by how people develop a sense of place. The Ockwells occupy a cottage adjacent to the original Paradise House, which at a quick glance looks sorely in need of renovation. They have three young daughters, who go to school at Glenorchy each week day.

Paradise has been run by a charitable trust since the death in 1998 of David Miller, the last owner, who wanted it to remain open for people to enjoy the forest and wildlife. Visitors rent the wooden huts and small cottages dotted about leafy parts of the property, the smaller ones looking like public works single men's quarters. All rentable units have a backblocks summer-holiday character, BYO everything.

Before being shown my hut for the night, I chat with Geoff about Paradise. Yes, there are plans not only to do up the old house and its annexe of guest rooms but also to expand the educational horizons of Paradise. Phys-ed students from Otago have come here for camps since the early 1970s. So have students from the University of South Australia, Adelaide. Geoff is engaged as an instructor for these camps, which teach outdoor pursuits skills. It's a haven for the young and the restless — and many other things besides.

William Mason, pioneer architect in New Zealand and first Mayor of Dunedin (1865–66), clearly saw its potential. He was seventy-three when he

Front-door knocker at Paradise House, featuring a musical cherub.

bought the property in 1883, a couple of years after Fenn acquired Arcadia. In fact, Fenn sold the 317 acres to William Mason. Herein lies an interesting personal link. Mason's second wife, Kate, had been married to an uncle of Fenn's, who died at the age of thirty-three. The Masons lived at Queenstown for six years before they developed Paradise, and during those years Kate must have mentioned the Head of the Lake, its farming and natural charms, to her nephew in England. Fenn beat the Masons to the Paradise area but the Masons quickly made it their place, too, building a fine homestead in the first year, with rooms for guests. There was a smoking room near the front of the house for the gentlemen, a sitting room opposite and a little room farther in that served as a post office, complete with its own Paradise postage stamp. In the entrance hallway were two glass cases containing mounted specimens of rare New Zealand birds, a kākāpō and a crested grebe.

The Masons soon established the property as a farm, introducing sheep, cattle, pigs, poultry and crops of oats and barley. They called their bucolic bolt-hole Eden Grove, after William's first home in Auckland. Conveniently, the name was a play on the Paradise theme. William Mason, born in England, achieved eminence as an architect after emigrating to New Zealand, a brand-new colony, from New South Wales in 1840.

At Paradise, his hiring of David and Jane Aitken as farm assistants boosted the guest-house reputation of the place. The Aitkens became lessees in 1891 then outright owners of the property in 1893, changing the name to Paradise House. For the next forty years they established it as a landmark of hospitality. Visitors came from far and wide. They took the steamer to Glenorchy and horse-drawn buggy up the road to the Rees Valley, across the chilly and not-always-safe river and on to the forest by Diamond Lake, where they passed through Heaven's Gate. At Paradise House, Jane Aitken might welcome visitors, depending on the time of day, with home-grown raspberries and Devonshire cream (which she made by setting pans of milk in a warm oven overnight), or hot scones with jam made from red currants, black currants or gooseberries, again all from the garden. Espaliered pear and apple trees bordered the pathway to the front door, and around the garden were drifts of columbines, lilies and pansies. Paradise had its own little school (now in use as a holiday hut), and a scheelite mine around the corner.

Guests came for the scenery and wildlife in this proverbial back of beyond. A stirring dawn chorus would be filled with the voices of many birds — the trilling sweet song of flocking yellowheads or mohua, which the British settlers called bush canaries; melodies from tūī and bellbird, the liquid calls and screeches of the forest parrot, kākā, and the undulating, wistful song, in a minor key, of the 'rain bird', the grey warbler or riroriro.

Perhaps, too, a guest with an uncommon interest in birdlife might recognise the 'bong' call of the South Island kōkako, the orange-wattled crow, and arrive at the breakfast table with terribly exciting news — how rare it was, the guest might say, to hear a native crow in southern districts; rarer still to see one. Of all the song birds of the New Zealand forest, the South Island kōkako was considered the most secretive. Predominantly lilac-grey, with conspicuous orange, fleshy lobes or wattles appended at the base of the beak on each side of the gape, it is more like the Australian apostlebird than a crow, and close to the dimensions of a magpie, although not as heavy. A black mask across the kōkako's face spans the eyes above the bill. It could be the avian equivalent of a 'Venetian' mask, such is the mystery and intrigue surrounding the bird today.

The Austrian naturalist and collector, Andreas Reischek, who spent several months in Fiordland in the 1880s, called it 'a master of hiding'.

Across the Main Divide, in South Westland, a kōkako population almost certainly lurked when Paradise House and Arcadia were in their heyday. The Head of the Lake, the forested arc from the Greenstone Valley around to the Rees, was an eastern frontier for the bird, with large tracts of forest giving way to tussock rangeland east of here, where the weak-flighted kōkako could not go.

Art, however, might have engrossed visitors to Paradise more than ornithology. Some guests were well-known painters, among them the Auckland-based landscape specialist, Charles Blomfield, who wrote about the coach ride from Glenorchy: '… caught in a thunderstorm, made for a house in the distance'. This was Paradise House, which he found to be 'furnished with grace and comfort'. The Masons imported walnut veneer furniture from England for the house in the wilds. Some photographers brought cumbersome glass-plate cameras, housed in large wooden boxes with black skirts attached, to capture the scenery, and writers kept journals that might one day form the basis of a novel.

Novelist Isabel Maud Peacocke, in *The House at Journey's End*, relates a love story about an Auckland woman, jilted in love, who travels to Paradise for a winter adventure and finds love again. '… a paradise it is to those who like scenery and plenty of it, snow-covered peaks, frost-bitten lakes, ice, rivers, beech forests, mist and rain and snow, icicles on the bushes …' What would Fenn have made of it? He rarely left Arcadia and died the year before the book was published, 1925.

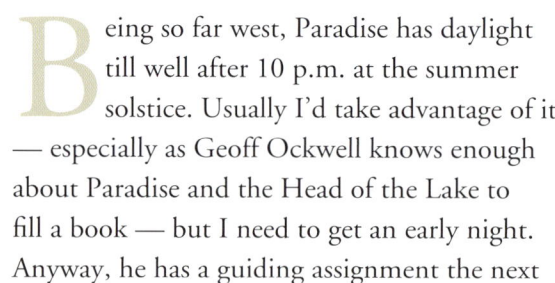

Being so far west, Paradise has daylight till well after 10 p.m. at the summer solstice. Usually I'd take advantage of it — especially as Geoff Ockwell knows enough about Paradise and the Head of the Lake to fill a book — but I need to get an early night. Anyway, he has a guiding assignment the next day for some visitors staying at the Blanket Bay Lodge near Glenorchy. Before heading for my hut, I wander around to the front door of the fabled Paradise House. Its frontage has seen better days, for sure. But the old horse chestnut tree is still there. Geoff tells me there are masses of polyanthus, in colourful, sweet profusion, under the tree in spring, and dainty white-tailed deer munch on the fallen chestnuts in autumn. These deer, introduced to the area in 1905 from New Hampshire, USA, live within about a twenty kilometre radius of Paradise. Leaping fences, they may leave their usual haunts in the beech forest to graze Arcadia's paddocks with the sheep and Simmental cattle during the day. Here the deer are protected.

My overnight accommodation is set back into the forest about 150 metres from Paradise House. It is a red-brown weatherboard unit in a clearing called 'Bushvedlt', a South African term a long way from home. The hut's commodious main room is equipped with a coal range, kitchen area, and two single beds, and there is a shower and porch off it. On the West Coast, you might hear such a dwelling described as a 'hut-house'. I whip up a quick brew on my gas cooker under candlelight, for the beech forest has wrapped the little clearing in a premature dusk, and retire to my sleeping bag.

Paradise, I soon discover, has things that move in the night. A tiny nip on my ear suggests an insect; scuffling noises suggest something larger. Mice! When the beech trees seed, as they have done this year, mice in plague numbers are usually the result. Now they are clattering about the hut, and I catch some of them in the beam of my torch. Perhaps driven by the hunger created by overpopulation, they are not the least bit scared of a visitor rustling in a sleeping bag. One or two scamper over the bottom of the bag.

I recall reading about a plague of rats encountered by the very first Europeans to reside and work at the Head of the Lake. Alfred Duncan, a Scottish shepherd assigned to look after the stock on the first sheep run, in the Rees Valley in 1861, told of rats eating their ropes, tobacco and practically anything not made of metal. 'They swarmed over us at night … we several times were aroused by their pulling at our hair.'

The rodent ruckus in Bushveldt eventually gets to me. I retreat to my Mazda wagon parked nearby, lowering the backseats so I can stretch out. It is worth the move just to experience the high-country starlight. Orion is angling its famous belt of stars towards a ragged skyline. Stars and silence, blessed relief. Then I hear mice again. Busy as ever, they are scrambling up the tyres and, by the sound of it, rummaging around under the bonnet. I will see in the morning whether they have disabled my transport by gnawing through electric wires. I'd like to be away early for Sugarloaf Pass.

Film-maker's darling

Paradise has been the darling of various film-makers in recent decades. In *The Lord of the Rings* films, the mossy forest of Lothlórien, filled with dappled light, was up the farm road from Paradise, at Dan's Paddock, and Boromir died in an area of forest close to Paradise House, called Amon Hen (pictured below). Narnia's *Prince Caspian* and a drama, *Vertical Limit*, also made use of the mountains and the forest, as did a fantasy movie called *Wolverine*, part of the *X-Men* series. But Paradise has had some of its charm knocked off during the making of these films, with a mess made in some of the moss gardens, and helicopter noise a nuisance to residents.

CHAPTER 2

Sugarloaf Pass

'A very curious circumstance'

Mr Buchanan, of the Geological Survey, has mentioned to me a very
curious circumstance frequently observed by himself at Otago: he has
seen these birds travelling through the bush on foot, Indian fashion,
sometimes as many as twenty of them in single file, passing rapidly over
the ground by a succession of hops, and following their leader like a
flock of sheep; for, if the first bird should have occasion to leap over a
stone or fallen tree in the line of march, every bird in the procession
follows suit accordingly!

From Sir Walter Buller's notes on South Island kōkako,
A History of the Birds of New Zealand, 1888

Around seven o'clock in the evening, two days after the 1995 summer
solstice, a graduate student from Harvard University, Cagan
Sekercioglu, who is of Turkish descent, crossed the swing-bridge at
the start of the Routeburn Track from the Glenorchy end, and set off at a brisk
pace for the camping spot at Routeburn Flats. He was alone. The weather was
clear, the light good.

He had hiked about a quarter of an hour and was close to the second swing-
bridge, which crosses Sugarloaf Stream, when he saw a bird close to the track,

low down. It was about twenty metres away. A bird biologist and wildlife photographer, Cagan knew he was looking at something different to what the guidebooks told him to expect in these southern forests. The bird, a dark-grey shape in the twilight, made no sound, and the forest itself was quiet. As he reached for his binoculars, the bird moved farther away from the track. But it stayed within his line of sight and he got a clear view of it for a few moments before it was gone.

'When I first saw it,' Cagan wrote in an 'incident report' for the Department of Conservation a few days later, 'I thought it was a huia.' But then he remembered huia were extinct, and anyway, they were North Island birds. The reason he thought of huia first was because of the 'prominent orange wattles' on the bird (huia had orange wattles, as do South Island kōkako). He'd already seen saddlebacks, a related wattle bird, on his travels in New Zealand and knew he wasn't looking at a saddleback. It had to be a South Island kōkako, the only other possibility among the ancient family of New Zealand wattle birds. He knew it was rare if not extinct. It was, he wrote, using the scientific name for the family, 'definitely a callaeid'.

Cagan continued on to the Routeburn Flats, pitched his tent there and wondered what to do about what he'd just seen. When I contacted him several years later, by which time he had a Ph.D. from Stanford University in the causes and consequences of bird extinctions in tropical countries, and was working as a bird conservation specialist with a long list of projects to his name, he recalled having doubts about whether he should report the Sugarloaf Stream sighting. He was worried he might be regarded as an attention-seeking 'stringer' — a foreigner to boot. 'Stringer' is an American term for a birdwatcher who fakes sightings of rare birds.

In the end, his conscience was tweaked. He decided that he couldn't ignore the conservation implications of not reporting a kōkako in the Routeburn area. Moreover, he would have felt, as he put it, 'very guilty not mentioning it'. After completing the Routeburn tramp he contacted the Department of Conservation office in Dunedin, the government agency responsible for protecting endanger-ed species, and wrote out the incident report. Cagan had come to New Zealand at the end of a three-month project in the World Heritage rainforest of the Atherton Tablelands, Northern Queensland, and returned to the United States to continue his studies and an international career in bird conservation.

The 1995 Sugarloaf Stream sighting is significant. For a start, it is relatively recent in the sketchy history of the species, reports of which pepper the records of rare-bird sightings through the last half of the twentieth century. The Department of Conservation (DOC) believes the South Island kōkako is gone for good. In January 2007, a DOC report stated there had been 'no confirmed sightings for forty-five years'.

That statement is questionable. The pivotal word is 'confirmed'. There have been numerous 'sightings' (but no photographs of sufficient clarity) and reports of distinctive calls in recent decades. Although there hasn't been enough evidence to convince the classifiers of threatened species at the Department, applying the designation 'Extinct' is a big call.

Of several reliable sightings in the twentieth century, a stand-out is the report by a deerstalker, K. McBride, of two sightings in successive years, 1966–67, in the same area of the little-visited Tiel Valley near Makarora, north of Lake Wanaka. In May 1966, the hunter saw a kōkako on a branch at the edge of beech forest. He reported 'putty coloured' wattles and a black face. 'One could imagine it wearing a mask,' he said. The second sighting, in April 1967, was of a kōkako walking along a sloping log: '… it climbed the trunk in a most peculiar way. With each rather ungainly step upwards, it appeared to hold on to the bark with its beak, take a look at me, take another step … till it reached branches, when it hopped rapidly out of sight.' Several years later, an expedition that included officers from the Wildlife Service and the Department of Scientific and Industrial Research (DSIR) Ecology Division failed to locate any birds.

More recently, through the 1980s and 1990s, sporadic sightings or calls indicative of kōkako have been reported from the Wakatipu region — from the valleys bounding the Head of the Lake, the Greenstone, Caples, Routeburn, Earnslaw Burn and Rees. A scatter of reports — sightings, calls and kōkako-like moss grubbings, first noticed in the Tiel Valley incidents — emanated from expeditions made into the Upper Caples in 1983–84 by a group of dedicated ornithologists, including Peter Child and Rhys Buckingham. They knew what to listen and look out for. Other reports were from people without an educated eye or ear for kōkako but who clearly heard, and sometimes saw, something unusual. Cagan Sekercioglu's sighting near Sugarloaf Stream falls somewhere between 'expert' and 'non-expert'. Although he was a student at the time, his experience and academic achievements have since multiplied, and no one would deny his credibility now.

Moss-laden windfall in beech forest.

In all, the evidence points to the real possibility that kōkako, in very small numbers and widely distributed, were surviving in forests at the Head of the Lake towards the turn of the century. With all this in mind, and a trip to Sugarloaf Pass in prospect, I thought I had better familiarise myself with kōkako calls.

The 'go to' man on South Island kōkako vocalisations is John Kendrick, now living at Waipu, just south of Whangarei. I have met Johnny a number of times. A sound recordist with the New Zealand Wildlife Service for twenty years, and the originator of the bird calls you hear on the hour during Radio New Zealand National's Morning Report, he is one of nature's most ardent enthusiasts. An animated fellow, now well into his eighties, Johnny shows little sign of slowing down. He talks as if his mind is whirring like a tūī's wingbeat. Recent excursions are his favourite topic. When I phone to ask if he could send me any recordings of South Island kōkako calls, he tells me excitedly about his recent ascent (his third in a year, with botanists) of a 400-metre hill overlooking Whangarei Harbour. Certainly Johnny has done the hard yards in the wilds of New Zealand, lugging heavy sound-recording equipment into some pretty remote places.

And it's not easy keeping up with impassioned bird researchers on the trail of the obscure. Rhys Buckingham is among them — my choice for an 'iron man of ornithology' award if ever such a thing is created. Based at Mapua in the Nelson region, Rhys has made the rediscovery of South Island kōkako his mission in life. His first glimpse of a South Island kōkako was on Stewart Island in 1977 in a tributary of the Freshwater River below Mount Anglem. He saw the bird — a 'large, longish-tailed grey bird' — after hearing a penetrating and melodic call during steady rain, when most birds go silent. The kōkako sang from high up in the canopy of mature rimu trees. Before he confirmed the call as coming from a kōkako he thought it sounded like a mixture of tūī and bellbird notes. In the 1980s he and Johnny Kendrick journeyed into the Upper Caples, Stewart Island and Northwest Nelson in search of kōkako.

The kōkako calls on Morning Report are of the North Island kōkako, which survives in viable numbers with the assistance of a recovery programme. Rarely have the calls of the South Island bird been recorded. I'm told the calls of the two birds differ. I expect Johnny's collection of the southern bird's calls to include some of the more bizarre sounds. On the phone, he apologises to me in advance for the tape's background noise and lack of clarity.

'Quality's not the best,' he says. 'The recording equipment wasn't as good

Classical peaks

Names from Greek and Roman mythology proliferate in the Humboldt Mountains and along the Main Divide in this area, among them Cosmos, Somnus, Minos, Mercury, Apollo, Nox, Nereus, Poseidon, Amphion, Niobe, Erebus, Chaos and Pluto.

These are the mountains of the gods, the mountains of myth.

Some of them — Cosmos and Somnus, for example — were named by James McKerrow, who led reconnaissance surveys through the region in 1862–63. A Scotsman, McKerrow was assigned by his boss, the Chief Surveyor of Otago, John Turnbull Thomson, to go and fill 'the blank on the map' known as the southern lakes district.

Over time, more names of Greek and Roman gods and mythological figures were attached to these mountains. Arcadia Station founder Joseph Fenn produced a few of these names. Some have been officially gazetted after deliberation by the New Zealand Geographic Board, others have the status of 'recorded names' — that is, they appear on maps and have become accepted by general usage but have yet to be gazetted, and the proposers of these names, settlers and mountaineers perhaps, are not easily identified.

Given his brief to fill a 'blank', McKerrow may not have known that Māori overlanders had their own names for the peaks, some of them representing spiritual beings. The highest peaks between the Dart Valley and the Beans Burn he named Cosmos, from a Greek word meaning an ordered whole or system and a synonym today for the universe. Pre-European Māori knew the same mountains as Koroka. From a certain place on the Dart River, the skyline of Koroka took the shape of a giant's face lying down — a landmark of immense significance to these early people. It guided them to the source of their most precious stone, pounamu/greenstone.

Mountain ranges such as Humboldt and Forbes were named by James McKerrow after distinguished men of science. Alexander von Humboldt (1769–1859) was a Prussian naturalist and explorer who travelled in Latin America and inspired the discipline of biogeography. His crowning literary work was called *Cosmos*. James David Forbes was a professor of natural philosophy at Edinburgh University from 1833 to 1860.

as you get these days. That, and the calls were sometimes coming from a fair way off. I'll send you a tape tomorrow.' Not one to mess about, is Johnny.

The cassette tape arrives in the post. The calls run for about ten minutes. Johnny's voice announces the collection as 'Calls of presumed South Island kōkako'. Applying scientific caution, he puts an emphasis on the word, 'presumed'. He has never seen and heard a South Island kōkako at the same time. He saw the 'tail end' (feathers fanned) of a bird in flight, presumed to be a kōkako, in Stewart Island's Freshwater River catchment in the 1980s. But he has heard some amazing things, and the cassette tape he has sent me contains them, each sequence preceded by an announcement of the place and month of the recording. They are all from the 1980s — from the Caples Valley, Stewart Island and Rocky River, which is in Kahurangi National Park, northwest Nelson.

The 'bong' call is up first, from the Caples Valley in December 1983. It is among the first calls ever recorded of South Island kōkako, certainly the first that Johnny ever heard. Rhys Buckingham was with him that day, and saw how the call immediately 'transformed' Johnny. Listening to the resonance of the taped single note over and above a background hiss and the calls of other birds, I find it remarkable. It is the call with the most 'carry' of any forest bird. Rhys reported such calls as carrying more than a kilometre in the right acoustic conditions. Kōkako surveys in the Caples around this time identify features such as the 'Kōkako Tree', where birds were seen, and calls were recorded by Johnny, and Callaeas Flat, named by Peter Child after the kōkako family name and a bunch of sightings there. One such sighting was by Peter himself: in which he described a bird running 'in giant strides' up the leaning trunk of a mountain beech tree — clearly not a blackbird and too long-legged to be kākā. On elegant legs, kōkako run, bound and hop — the 'squirrels' of the New Zealand forest.

The next calls on John Kendrick's tape, recorded on Stewart Island, are rather more difficult to describe. For one of these calls, delivered as a couplet, imagine two solid sticks being knocked together and lay that sound over the top of the short, sharp screech of a pūkeko. Then there is a sound somewhere between a staccato bark and a cough or grunt: a series of half a dozen short, deeply delivered 'huh, huh' sounds that rise and fade away. To make sure Johnny has not mixed up bird calls with the noises made by an animal — what I have in mind are exotic animals from, say, the South American jungles! — I phone him.

'Yes, sticks banged together — that's pretty close to it,' he says.

'And the barking?'

'Maybe.'

'Johnny, could Stewart Island's white-tailed deer be making these sounds?' I am flailing around for an animal to blame.

'Perhaps it could. But show me a deer that can get thirty feet up a rimu tree. That's where the sound was coming from. Couldn't see the bird.'

'A possum then?'

'I doubt it. This was daytime, and possums don't really make sounds like that in daylight hours. Did you hear the swinging gate calls?' says Johnny.

I'm not sure whether I did or not. I'm flummoxed enough as it is.

The tape goes on to deliver a descending three-note melody, with the last note repeated — rather tūī-like — and another series of chime-like calls with harmonic qualities sweet to the ear. There are bellbird alarm calls going off at the same time. These alarm calls are rowdy when you hear them in person in the forest but now, on this tape, much less powerful than the 'presumed kōkako' chimes. I am reassured. I am also now thinking that when it comes to the sounds they make, South Island kōkako are off the planet.

After a rodent-ridden night in the Bushveldt at Paradise, I drive around to the Routeburn Valley. The weather is holding fine. You enter Mount Aspiring National Park to get to the start of the Routeburn Track, one of New Zealand's most popular alpine treks. It's a trampers' highway, walkable two abreast for most of the way. The Sugarloaf Pass track, I'm guessing, will be less civilised. The turn-off for the pass is before you get to the stream. Cagan's kōkako sighting took place a little farther on from the turn-off. I'll have all ears open for swinging gates and animals coughing. Looking at the distance on the map and the 600 metre climb to the pass, I predict it will take me about two hours to make the Lark's rendezvous point at noon. I'm good for time.

Walking through red beech forest of the kind you encounter at the start of the Routeburn Track is a magnificent experience. You stroll among giants — huggable but impossible to get your arms around. High up, their foliage is more open, airy and carefree than that of the podocarps, rimu and totara, and a lighter green. In a breeze they are scintillating. Moist podocarp forest is invariably a jungle; the beech forest understorey, typically sparse, is easier to negotiate, with carpets of moss and lichen softening the way. From logs and branches, miniature forests of beech seedlings sprout red-leafed progeny from the same seeding year.

I know this red beech experience won't last because these trees are not as hardy as mountain and silver beech, which are found higher up the mountain-sides, indeed all the way to the tree line. The reds, largest of the beech species, reaching a height of thirty metres, prefer lower elevations, moist but generally more fertile soils, and a reasonable climate.

The red beech is where the robins live. And falcons, it seems. Crossing the swing-bridge over the river at the track entrance, I fluked a fleeting view of a falcon — it looked like a young male — gliding on dappled, rounded wings down the river's avenue of beech trees, towards the mouth. My mind diverted to the Lark and his interest in falcons. I wonder which way he will come to get to the pass. There is a trail from the next valley, the Rock Burn.

I've been walking just a few minutes after crossing the swing-bridge, when a robin alights nearby on wings gossamer-quiet and legs as thin as match-sticks. Its close approach is astonishing. Few native or introduced birds are as confiding. This one flicks its bill at the leaf litter, bidding me do the same, it seems. Having been in robin habitat many times before, I oblige with my hands then draw back, knowing the bird will fly at once to the disturbance and feast its beady black eyes, with its head tipped, on whatever is crawling there. It pays to be pushy if you are a foraging robin; trouble is, its ground-foraging habit makes it vulnerable to rats and stoats. When I get back I'll try to find out whether the Routeburn robins are holding their own in the face of predation. They deserve to be. They have enchanted echelons of day-trippers and trampers since the first visitors explored the Routeburn on horseback in the 1880s.

It's a Friday, and the last day of the working year for most people. I have a head start on outdoor recreation this Christmas. Bright red plastic triangles, nailed to trees at intervals, mark the track, which is criss-crossed by tree roots and faint in places. It's a steady grade.

No, hurry — I'm all ears for bongs or the banging of sticks. The commonest calls are the chattering of the ubiquitous, introduced chaffinch and the softer voices of two native species: rifleman and grey warbler. The rifleman, smaller than mice and all but tail-less, was named by European settlers who thought their plumage resembled the colours of a rifle-toting colonial regiment. The grey warbler's nest could be filled at this time of year with a couple of shining cuckoo chicks that are bizarrely larger than the foster parents. A melodic call in the distance pulls me up, and my ears really are now on full alert — until I realise the song is coming from a tūī or perhaps a bellbird.

In half an hour I reach a ford above the junction of two branches of Sugarloaf Stream. For much of this first leg of the climb, the roar of the Routeburn charging through its gorge of boulders has been filtering through the forest canopy. The river's voice runs out more or less where the red beech trees disappear from the canopy, leaving the small-leaved mountain beech in charge. The oldest trees, red beech in particular, develop holes in their trunks that are suitable for nesting mohua/yellowheads and parakeets. The canary-yellow mohua, like the grey warbler, may host cuckoo eggs and chicks — in the mohua's case, not shining cuckoo but long-tailed cuckoo, which, uninvited, will present eggs for the mohua to hatch, and outsize chicks to raise.

The understorey here, above the red beech zone, is sparse: small prickly totara, flat-leaved celery pine, coprosma bushes and beech saplings that are canopy trees in waiting. They wait for a windfall, the felling by old age or windstorm of one of canopy trees. This creates a well of light and an inevitable growth spurt for the next generation of trees.

Not far above the ford I sit down to rest amid sunbeams penetrating the canopy. I take a drink and knot the corners of a handkerchief for a makeshift hat. Regrettably, my sunhat is back in the wagon. Being among the folliclely challenged, I will need some sort of protection from the sun when I get above the tree line.

Still seated on a bank of clubmoss, I glimpse a movement about five metres ahead, just off the track. It is a flicker, nothing more, and perhaps I am deceived by a falling leaf. The forest is hushed. No, there it is again. A furry face appears at the entrance to a hole that is a tight fit for it. I'm looking at a chestnut-brown head, popping black eyes and short ears curled forward. Stoat!

We eye each other. In an instant the face is gone. It is hard to believe the animal can back up so quickly. There it is again, momentarily, a puppet-head with whiskers: small, cute and deadly to just about every living thing in this forest: bird, mouse, rat, gecko, weta, beetle, even possum.

I ready my camera with a telephoto lens and lie propped on elbows, hoping for a shot. I wait for some minutes. The puppet show seems to be over.

I presume I have come upon a stoat at its den. You don't often see stoats in the forest. They are supremely clever and efficient hunters, able to climb trees,

Native daisy: a mountain celmisia in full bloom at Sugarloaf Pass, with the
Dart River in the distance.

manoeuvre in tight spaces, swim rivers, and outrun most things. Heart-lung rhythm is phenomenal — about one hundred breaths and an unbelievable 400 heartbeats a minute when at full stretch hunting. They live where they can find food. That means practically every habitat, wet or dry, hot or cold, between sea shore and alpine zone in the North and South Islands.

Stoats, in the same family as ferrets and weasels but more versatile and pervasive, are called ermine back in Europe and valued for their fur, white in winter. They were introduced into New Zealand from Britain in the 1880s to combat a rabbit plague in southern districts. The Wakatipu area received the first official lot to be imported. Stoats everywhere had government blessing and protection in the early years. Not so today. Stoats have paid much less attention to rabbits than to vulnerable native birds and other fauna. They have caused disastrous decline across an array of species. Falcons and feral cats are about their only predators in the wild, and a cat might rather choose to stalk a bird before bothering with a wily stoat.

I continue on my way. The canopy grows thinner and the forest floor is better lit, with low-stature silver beech replacing mountain beech towards the tree line. Silver beech predominates at the tree line through southern New Zealand, a species tolerant of snow, icy temperatures and the high rainfall. An exceptionally hardy tree, silver beech, and near the tree line it is festooned with pale-green old man's beard lichen, called Usnea, giving the forest a ghostly touch, especially in misty conditions. The sun beats down on the lichens now, evoking a fairyland rather than a hall of ghosts.

The tree line is a place worth savouring, a natural boundary where, typically, life revs up. Birds chase increased insect life, and the riflemen are plentiful on this Sugarloaf Pass section of the tree line today. I see a couple of tomtits and a bellbird. I hear parakeets and, distantly, a kea.

Then another surprise. Someone is coming down the track towards me. It's not the Lark. This guy is too tall, too clean-shaven. With designer sunglasses, a woollen shirt that looks newly purchased, and a bright-blue pack, he could be stepping out of a Queenstown hotel to go for a day hike up Ben Lomond. The tramper is German. He tells me he camped just down from the pass last night after being dropped off by the Dart Jet where the Rock Burn meets the Dart River. He planned to do a loop up the Rock Burn Valley and over Sugarloaf Pass to the Routeburn, where he expected to camp the night. But the climb to the pass took him longer than he expected — 'It was not like the German woods, it was hard' — and in cool, drizzly weather he was benighted on the pass.

'I was a bit, aah, nerved by the conditions,' he says in tentative English. 'No good place for my tent. And there was a mouse …'

'A mouse?'

'Yes, a mouse in my sleeping bag in the morning. It must have come in when I went out for a pee in the night. It ran out when I got up for breakfast.'

'Lucky mouse,' I say, 'getting warm lodgings for the night.' I want to share with him my overnight experience of marauding mice but think I shouldn't try to top his story. He is keen to keeping moving anyway and perhaps warm himself up, and I need to continue on my way, too, aware that my midday rendezvous time is rushing up.

Above the forest, there is a shrubland of juniper-scented manuka, orange-berried coprosma bushes, green skull-caps of subalpine hebe, filmy ferns and swathes of snow tussock grasses. The track is now a route marked by steel fence standards painted orange. It is muddy in places. Large white celmisia daisies, with prominent yellow centres and thick leaves that are furry underneath, appear amongst the tussocks — a sure sign of an alpine environment.

Catching my eye off the trail, in a bare patch among the tussocks, is a faded yellow object, foreign to these surroundings. My first thought is that it could be a discarded piece of bread or toast left behind by the German camper. It turns out to be the plastic lid of a can of Sustagen, the powder base for an American energy drink. I remember it from the 1970s and 1980s, and marathon running. The can, rusty now and squashed flat, has been here a long time. The brand name imprinted on the lid is only just legible. I leave it there, historic refuse. Carry out all you take in — that's the imperative today, especially in remote places like this. At least someone, way back then, felt compelled to squash the can, and reduce the footprint.

I can see a dip in the skyline where the pass must be. I am going to be a bit late, maybe ten minutes.

Sugarloaf Pass pulls into view. It arches smoothly from the Routeburn side to the Rock Burn, allowing a tramper to transit quickly between one valley and the other. Any mountain pass or saddle newly encountered is always a discovery, and, for me, as impressive as arriving at a summit. The surprise element is often on the cards. At the Cascade Saddle near the head of the Dart Valley on a fine afternoon a few years ago, I came upon a group of German women trampers stretched out in a grassy basin, enjoying the alpine sun —

topless. And a little farther on, three men in kilts wandered up from the Matukituki side on weary legs, bound for Dart Hut. They were card-carrying members — the leaders in fact, from Hamilton — of the McGillicuddy Serious Party, which added a 'Great Leap Backwards' brand of creativity and levity to general elections in the 1990s.

Yes, passes can sometimes funnel offbeat experiences. The Sugarloaf's natural doorway is far from dramatic. There are no bluffs or towering tors, just a tawny fur coat of snow tussock, with low shrubs of Dracophyllum interspersed. Sugarloaf Pass looks decidedly lonesome under a high sun. High noon, summer solstice.

'Long time, no sea lions!'

The voice — and there is no mistaking either voice or message — comes at me from one of the few schist outcrops in the pass, a hundred metres off to the left. In that direction, on the distant skyline, is one of the signal peaks of the northern Humboldt Mountains: Momus, which my research into the landmark names around here tells me is the Greek God of Ridicule!

I haven't seen the Lark since the sea lion episode at Taieri Mouth around the millennium summer. Now, sitting on tussocks beside a sloping grey rock the size of a musterer's hut, he seems much the same: ginger complexion, a touch lighter perhaps (and presumably ginger hair under his hat), pale-blue eyes and a few days' growth of whiskers. The blue denim cap of the Strath Taieri days has given way to an oilskin canvas hat, Southern Man style, with a brim to fend off the high-country sun as well as serious rain. He's wearing a black Swanndri, sleeveless out of respect for summer temperatures, I guess. His trousers look serviceable, made of moleskin or similar material. On his feet are calf-length gumboots, the lace-up kind but modified with two short lengths of wire instead of laces binding the eyelets — a durable invention, good for wet going or rocky places, sturdy enough for long stretches, and convenient if you want to get into and out of the boots in a hurry.

'Solstice greetings,' I say, searching for a line appropriate to the occasion.

'Yeah, sun's all downhill from today,' says the Lark. 'Take a pew.' I nestle into the tussock. He tips back his hat. 'This beats the Christmas rush, eh? You got my invitation, then.'

'Sure did. I'm intrigued. A new lair for the Lark, is it?'

Instead of answering my question, he has one of his own that threatens to invoke Momus. 'Nice hat. Where'd you get it?'

'Left the real one in the car. It's not going to be much protection if a falcon attacks me.'

I tell him about the notice I'd seen at the DOC office in Glenorchy warning trampers to look out for dive-bombing falcons on the Rees-Dart Track, particularly at Shelter Rock and Cattle Flat. The notice cautioned trampers to 'avoid injury' without saying how exactly. Recalling images of his hang-gliding pastime in the Strath Taieri and his aerial connection with a falcon called Freefall, I ask, 'Tried any of your gliding stuff in this area?'

'Nope. The forest makes things a bit tricky here. Winds are unpredictable, too. You should see what it's like when a decent storm hits. Besides, the years are piling up on me. Better off walking these days. How about a bite to eat?'

From my day-pack I haul out home-made sandwiches and some fruit. As the Lark reaches for his supplies, he says: 'Hope you're set for tucker. I'm a sandwich short of a picnic.'

There is much to catch up on with the Lark, and in the circumstances, food seems like a minor and mechanical detail, a refuelling. Falcons are still on my mind. I tell him about the bird I saw gliding down the Routeburn this morning. No doubt he knows something about the falcons in this area. He starts telling me about a falcon nest he discovered near the bridge to Lake Sylvan, three kilometres downstream of the Routeburn Track entrance.

'It was under a log.'

'A log? Wouldn't that be unusual?'

'Too true. For this area anyhow. The nest was on the ground, nothing more than flattened grass tucked under the thick end of the log. The pair was smart enough to know the site was protected from rains from the north. They raised a couple of young.'

The Lark says that apart from the fact it was at ground level, the nest site had the dimensions of a rock ledge on a schist outcrop, with a view south over a paddock where the Sylvan sawmill operated in the 1920s. The Central Otago rangeland falcons favour nest sites on cliffs or at the base of overhanging rocks. They like settings people pay big money for — a view with water in it.

'Round here,' the Lark says, 'falcons generally build their nests in the trees. But not this pair. Guess that's nature for you. As soon as you think you've got nature worked out, she'll contradict you, throw up something strange and unheard of. That, I like. Around nature you can't sound too certain of your facts, or too much of a know-all. You could get your theories blown away.'

'Know-all' is certainly not a label I'd put on the Lark. He's a practical guy, in touch with the land. I know him as a musterer with dog at heel, a general farm hand and a shearer, too. He even does water divining for farmers during dry spells on the Strath Taieri. Not much call for that talent in the Head of the Lake area. Rainfall is pretty well assured, and the rivers run steadily. So what kind of life does he have in this region?

'Are you going to tell me what you're doing here?'

'Bits and pieces,' says the Lark, dismissively. 'Tell you what, let's get moving. I'll show you some of the sights.'

'Okay, but I'll need to be heading back in a couple of hours. My family want me back for Christmas. What are your plans?'

'Show you in a mo, when we get higher.'

We pack up the lunch things. The Lark rehooks his gumboots. I'm aware of a northerly breeze fanning the pass — little more than a puff. But it may be signalling a change in the mild, pleasant weather. There's a build-up of high cloud in the north and west, where the heavy-duty clouds and rain mostly come from. For the moment, though, the tops are clear, the views jaunty to say the least.

North of the lunch spot, through the dish that is the pass, the peaks rising to Mt Nox, Roman Goddess of the Night, are lined out on the other side of the Rock Burn Valley, surprisingly close in the mountain air. Their steepness is evident from the rock screes spilling into the gullies and from the waterfalls — vertical silver threads through the dark skirt of forest. White splotches around the tops suggest the spring snows might have run into summer. I know from the map that Mt Nox and its cohort, Minos, who was an ancient King of Crete, conceal one of the region's highest alpine lakes. With the tantalising name of Lake Unknown, it occupies a cold, cliff-bound crucible at the same elevation as Sugarloaf Pass. I've heard it is a very steep climb from the Beans Burn, and may have to remain unknown to me.

'This way,' says the Lark.

We leave the poled route, heading east in the direction of the Dart Valley. Mount Earnslaw and Turret Head dominate the skyline. I can see immediately the Lark is still a smart mover through tussock country. He walks with an even, gliding motion.

There are faint animal tracks through the grassland as we climb a spur. I start up a hare from under a tussock, a creature not often associated with the low-alpine zone. It's huge — the size of a fox — and bounds away till it is out of sight. The plant life becomes more diverse the higher we go, with the snow grasses now competing for space with native edelweiss and buttercups, celmisia daisies, snowberry, white lichens and multi-coloured cushion plants.

Across an open patch a pipit, crying 'scree', runs off in a jerky manner with its tail flicking nervously. These native birds, typically found in rangeland and low-alpine zones but occupying other habitats as well, are often mistaken for the introduced skylark, and vice-versa. The birds are similar in size and colour, mottled buff brown with creamy streaks, and both build simple nests on the ground, lined with grass, lichens and other camouflaging vegetation. The pipit is the more slender of the two. It also has a distinctive dark stripe through the eye area. I remember the Lark — his mispronunciation of Alec when he was a child — informing me during his hang-gliding days in the Strath Taieri that the collective name for a group of larks is an exaltation. Perhaps a group of pipits might be called a 'palpitation' on account of their flicking tails.

'That's the Rock Burn,' says the Lark.

Puffing a little, and noticing the Lark exhibiting no sign of having climbed through the herbfields and grasslands, I look back. The straight middle reach of the Rock Burn is picturesquely laid out. Glacier ice, not water, carved the valley — large-scale landscaping — before departing in rather a hurry, say, 12,000 years ago, as the climate warmed. The Rock Burn is a sizeable river, and beech forest cuddles it through this reach except for a grassy river flat that the Lark is now pointing out.

'Blue ducks live there,' he says. 'They've gone from a lot of places now but the pair down there seem to be holding on. The yellowheads are mostly this side of the patch of river flats you can see. Kākā love the place, too.'

'You seem to have a good handle on the birdlife.'

'Yeah, at times I work with the conservation crowd. Volunteer for the yellowhead monitoring stuff. Bit of stoat trapping, that sort of thing. There's a line of traps through the whole of the Rock Burn, right up to the basin under Park Pass. Hens' eggs for bait. Someone's got to check the traps every few months. Up the top end they're protecting blue ducks; yellowheads at the bottom. Kākā, too. Gets me out and about, this caper. Yeah, I'm on the "super" now — a superant. Bloody marvellous, having the taxpayer fund my lifestyle.'

Yes, the Lark is certain to have low overheads — and he hasn't got much need for infrastructure, either. From what he tells me, there are rock shelters in most valleys that are dry and inviting, with a north-facing one beneath an overhang at Theatre Flat exceptionally good for a night or two. Despite his advancing years he seems in good shape for an outdoor life.

His knowledge of local birds has me thinking he might have heard of kōkako sightings in the past, maybe even the 1995 record from the Sugarloaf catchment.

'A long shot, I know, but what's your opinion on the kōkako? There was a reported sighting a few years back in the Sugarloaf Stream area.'

I am taken aback by his response.

'There's every chance they're still around. Won't be many left, mind. Mysterious bird, the kōkako. Likes to hide from people. I heard something in the Earnslaw Burn back in the 'eighties. A loud bonging bell sound that turned kind of mournful. It hung in the air like it was bouncing off the foliage. Seemed to stay with me for some time after the bird had stopped uttering it. Later on, there was a "crraaaww", repeated a few times. You'd swear it was an animal sound or a crow. I read they're related to crows.'

'Distantly, they are…'

'Never saw anything of the bird myself that time. A year or two before that, a couple of trampers from Otago, father and daughter, reckoned they came upon one in the Earnslaw Burn forest.'

The Lark describes what they saw — a greyish bird fitting the description of a kōkako. They'd stopped on the forest track for a rest when they suddenly realised there was a fairly large bird looking at them. It moved about the lower branches then disappeared. It had an 'apricot' splash of colour on it, presumably the wattles. The bird was silent the whole time.

'That would have been about nineteen seventy-nine,' says the Lark. 'Years later, the man climbed Mount Earnslaw — at the age of seventy-six, I heard. From what I know about kōkako, the chances of hearing and seeing a bird at the same time … well, you'd win Lotto before you'd strike that. Say, why don't I show you the Earnslaw Burn rock shelter in the new year? It's about the flashest starlight hotel in this area, right down to wire bed bases and mattresses these days.'

I tell him I could probably make it late February or March, if, somehow, he could phone or email me with a time and day. Communication is not a strong point of his. He has no fixed abode.

Meanwhile, a plane is buzzing somewhere overhead, bound for Milford from Queenstown no doubt. Bouncing off the valley walls, the engine noise is amplified and difficult to pinpoint. It's a well-worked tourist route, this one, with passengers willing to pay the extra dollars to get to Milford by air rather than the long haul by road. The Lark is looking upwards, too.

'Imagine,' he says, 'going non-stop from one lot of tarsealed busyness — Queenstown, that is — to another place that's also teeming with people, Milford. Suits me that they leave all this wilderness alone.'

Off to the south the Dart River's delta heaves into view. I can make out the road bridge over the river, and the hillocks nearby created by the Dart Glacier dumping separate loads of rock debris when its progress was stalled. The glacier, a remnant of its original size, has since retreated forty-five kilometres back into its snowfield cirque or head basin. On the far side of the Dart Valley from the Sugarloaf hills is the line of mountains flanking Paradise. We come to a couple of small alpine ponds and soon afterwards, on the other side of a low rise, there is a much larger tarn filling a curved basin, about 200 metres long. The north wind is ruffling its surface.

'That'll be far enough today,' the Lark says. 'But look out to the right. That's Sugarloaf. No time to get there now. The route crosses a couple of gullies. But it's a powerful place, a footstool for the mountain gods, I reckon. Like Smooth Cone in the Strath Taieri, it's got some energy associated with it. Know what I mean?'

'Intersecting lay lines, that sort of thing?' I say.

'Something like that … always feel pretty good going up these hills.'

There are certainly plenty of lines on any map around here, with Mount Aspiring and Fiordland National Parks sharing a boundary on the Main Divide. Both parks form a World Heritage site, as well. The Lark points out Park Pass at the head of the Rock Burn Valley. We can just make it out. White clouds are starting to spill over from the Hollyford catchment in Fiordland. There's rain on the way.

'Where are you headed now?' I ask.

'Back to the Rock Burn. People called the valley the Rocky Burn at one time. Reminds me of my old collie — remember him? Rocky, the black-and-white job. Best dog I ever had. Best co-pilot, too. Old age got to him during a muster, and I buried him by the hut. Being mostly up this way now and in the national park — dogs not permitted — I haven't bothered replacing him.'

'Sorry to hear that. He was your one-good-dog-in-a-lifetime dog, I think you said.'

The Lark says he's going to join a couple of young fellows doing a bird survey, then head out to one of the sheep stations for Christmas, probably after a night down at the hut by the Rock Burn mouth.

'Not much of a hut, that one. Dark hole of a place. But a roof in the rain. Rodents own it just now. There's a mouse plague.'

I tell him I've seen a few mice myself. But I'm more interested in his plan to spend Christmas on a high-country station. 'You'd be following in the footsteps of Arawata Bill, you know, doing that kind of thing. Have you heard of him? Bill O'Leary — prospector, bush ranger, legendary loner. He used to come out of the mountains for Christmas.'

'Sure I've heard of him. Relatives of mine talked of Arawata. They're the reason I'm here, the rellies.'

The Lark goes on to say he had an uncle on land near Glenorchy, and during school holidays in the 1950s he would visit him and his cousins, travelling up on the old lake steamer, Earnslaw. It made a change from schooling in Oamaru. The 'fifties are a bygone era, the likes of which Glenorchy will never see again. There was no road then.

But there is now, and I need to be on it soon enough. With the Earnslaw Burn rendezvous agreed, and another opportunity to hear more of the Lark's life after Middlemarch, I am glad we're turning back to the saddle.

My impressions of him as a man alone are confirmed — a man of mountains tall and sharp now, not of the hump-backed ranges of Central Otago. Except that 'man alone' seems a rather desolate and piteous image. 'Man alive!' is nearer the mark. He's still getting round the hills at a clip; still travelling light.` And still keen to keep in touch with me from time to time, it seems.

We diverge near the small tarns and begin angling back to meet our respective trails, one north, one south, both downhill. A few minutes later, I pass close to something shining amongst the tussocks. It's a map of the Dart/Routeburn area at 1:50,000 scale (one kilometre to twenty millimetres), protected by plastic lamination — an extraordinary find given the remote location. It has been folded twice for easy reference while backpacking. Did it belong to the German tramper? No, the water staining round the edges and the black mould suggest it has lain here for months, perhaps years.

Intriguingly, Sugarloaf Pass lies right at the centre of the folds. A hare or mouse has chewed a small hole clear through the map in the area near Lake Unknown. Paradise and the Earnslaw Glacier are on the right hand side; Lake

Harris and the Harris Saddle, which the Routeburn Track crosses into Fiordland, are on the left.

It is a mystery map, for sure. I take it as a souvenir. Maps are worth cherishing and poring over. Before printed maps in this country there were the oral maps of the Māori, with landmarks, including mountain peaks and river bends and confluences, remembered in song and chant — the land's first poetry. Early European explorers relied on Māori guides who knew those maps. It amazes me how long it took Europeans to find their way to the Wakatipu district following the settlement of Dunedin, coastal Otago and Southland — five years! It was late in 1853 when Nathanael Chalmers, an adventurous twenty-two-year-old Scots farmer and sheep importer, engaged two Māori guides from Southland, Reko and Kaikoura Whakatau, to show him the way inland to lakes that were roughly configured on white settlers' maps but which had never been seen by European eyes. Chalmers climbed the Hector Mountains after a few days' travel north from the Mataura area for a view he described as 'a lot of water and snowy mountains'. He was looking at Lake Wakatipu and the Alps beyond, known to moa-hunter Māori for centuries. It took the trio three weeks to make a 500-kilometre loop through the interior, taking in Lakes Wakatipu, Wanaka and Hawea. They completed it by rafting the Clutha River back to Balclutha, a heart-stopping experience through the gorges.

A modern topographical map at 1:50,000 scale (one kilometre to two centimetres) conveys a sense of place. It allows the reader to picture the lie of the land, and the nature of it, too, through symbols for forest, swamp, scree, cliffs, gravel bed, sand hill, ice and so on. Go to internet maps today, like Google Earth, and you can zoom into people's backyards and washing lines through powerful satellite images. You could argue there's too much definition: it's too much in your face. Imagination is stifled, and with it the prospect of adventure.

The map I retrieve from the furry embrace of the Sugarloaf tussock has an added and mysterious dimension: where had its owners come from, and where were they going? Apart from an animal's nibbling there are no marks on it.

The pass recedes behind me as I regain the forest. The day has grown dull and the breeze is a moderate gusty wind now. It causes the canopy to whisper in fits and starts and the branches of some trees to grind together. Although annoying to anyone listening out for bird calls, these are encouraging sounds for the forest's next generation of canopy trees, living a stunted life in the hope of a windfall.

'... departed spirits'

'The cry of the crow is indiscribably mournfull [sic]. The wail of the wind through a leafless forest is cheerful compared to it. Perhaps the whistling of the wind through the neck of an empty whisky bottle is the nearest approach to it, and is sadly suggestive of departed spirits.'

Charlie Douglas, bushman-explorer, South Westland
Journal entry, about 1890

South Island kōkako. Neville Peat/courtesy of Otago Museum

The river-flat pastures of Mount Earnslaw Station with the valley of the Earnslaw Burn in the background.

CHAPTER 3

Character Town

In the 1950s, when the Lark spent school holidays at the Head of the Lake, life was simple for Glenorchy folk. The days of the week were basically of two kinds — Boat Day and No Boat Day. On Boat Day, the steamer *Earnslaw*, approaching fifty years of age, pulled into the Glenorchy wharf accompanied by a plume of black coal smoke (she could burn a tonne of coal an hour) and the sound of the telegraph on the bridge dinging signals to the engine room. Brass fittings gleamed, and the ship listed as passengers pressed against her wharf-side rail to see who was at the wharf to meet them. Sometimes the whole village turned out, or so it seemed. There were three return sailings a week in summer, Monday, Wednesday and Friday, and two in winter, Monday and Friday. Depending on the number of calls at lakeside sheep stations, the trip would take about two hours one way.

With the road to Queenstown little more than a bridle track and stock route, the steamer service was the Head of the Lake's conduit to the outside world. Smaller and slower than the *Earnslaw*, another steamship, the *Ben Lomond*, alternated with the *Earnslaw* on the service before 1951. The *Ben Lomond*, formerly the *Jane Williams*, was withdrawn that year, leaving the *Earnslaw* as the only large vessel left for the run to Glenorchy and Kinloch on the opposite side of the lake. Glenorchy people were not sorry to see the *Ben Lomond*'s withdrawal from service. She had

scared the living daylights out of a fair number of them on trips that were unfortunate enough to encounter a severe northerly storm.

The way the Lark heard it from his uncle, the *Ben Lomond* was 'a bugger to pitch and roll'. In a really violent storm, no one could move around the ship as she battled up the north arm of the lake. The fetch of twenty-five kilometres, in storm-force winds, could generate waves over three metres high. The *Ben Lomond* would round White Point to face the waves bow on, and the propeller sent a shudder through the whole ship as it neared the surface whenever the bow dipped into a big trough. There was no turning back, no deviating to a station wharf along the way (Mount Creighton, Elfin Bay, Greenstone) — and no morning tea.

Typically, for morning tea, scones were served on the outward sailing, crackers and cheese on the return trip in the afternoon. The tea came in fine china, laid out on tables with a lip around the edge to stop the crockery falling off in rough weather. The chairs were bolted to the deck. These precautions, it should be noted, were for a passenger and freight vessel plying a body of fresh water — not the open ocean. Clearly, their owners and builders had respect for weather 'bombs'.

The Lark's cousins told him about their worst trip to Glenorchy. Not only was there no morning tea, the tea lady was lying flat on the floor so she wouldn't be tossed around. Most people were seasick. The captain, confined to the wheelhouse, slowed the ship's speed till they seemed to be barely making headway into the gale and spray. The cousins were cowered and frightened by the violence of the storm, the thunder and occasional lightning, and the violent response of the ship to it all. When their father realised the *Ben Lomond* was two hours late, he climbed the hill behind the town to see if there was any sign of the vessel. He feared a tragedy. The children were put to bed soon after they came down the gangway at Glenorchy, ashen-faced, on trembling legs.

In earlier decades, the steamships would bring women in furs and hats, and men in suits, some of whom were bussed to Paradise for a holiday at one or other of the famous guest houses.

When the Lark holidayed at Glenorchy in the 1950s, the run from Queenstown was undertaken by the *Earnslaw* and a fleet of smaller launches, *Meteors I*, *II* and *III*. The dreaded *Ben Lomond* had been scrapped. Students at distant boarding schools were usually given the Friday off — the last Friday of the term at least — so they could make the Friday sailings from Queenstown.

Meat and bread was delivered to Glenorchy on Boat Days, and the appetising, homely smell of freshly baked bread carried right through the interior of ship or launch. The bread was often still warm when it arrived at the Glenorchy wharf. Years earlier, an entrepreneurial Queenstown woman would bring a stock of clothing on the steamer — functional rather than fashion garments, intended for farm and outdoors use. She would set up shop at the Mount Earnslaw Hotel, a short walk from the wharf.

If Boat Day coincided with pay day for the scheelite miners, the town was in high spirits.

The Lark's uncle worked a scheelite mine on a part-time basis, helping his father, who held the miner's licence. Meeting his nephew from Waitaki Boys' High at the wharf one hot summer's day, when a northwesterly föhn wind was whipping up a dust storm on the Dart River delta and parching the back of the throat, he walked him home via the Mount Earnslaw Hotel.

'Are you dry?' he said. The young Lark nodded. So into the bar they went, never mind the underage issue, and the uncle ordered a 'pony', a five-ounce beer served in a glass with a tapered waist. It cost sixpence.

Six o'clock closing for pubs across New Zealand, the law at the time, was hardly ever observed at Glenorchy. The town had no resident policeman. Occasionally, a constable would arrive from Queenstown by boat, only to find everything in order because someone on the vessel had radioed ahead that the long arm of the law was about to reach out to Glenorchy.

A summer holiday at Glenorchy, for a teenage boy, was a riot compared to the disciplinary atmosphere of a boarding school. There were rabbits to shoot for the kitchen table and 'flappers', too — young paradise shelducks, not yet fledged — at the lagoons or on the river bed around New Year, when it was too late for the duck-shooting season and seemingly too early for trout. Instead of shooting the young paradise ducks, the boys might throw stones to herd them towards the reedy edge of the lagoons, where they could nab them by hand. The young Lark once saw someone shoot a falcon that had been harassing hens. He felt like querying the wisdom of that. Falcons were magnificent birds, agile in the air. Courageous, too. They could take on prey much larger than themselves, such as hens and black shags. At Glenorchy, where he was a visitor and a guest, he tended to keep his tongue. Besides, there was so much fun to be had with his cousins. There were boulders to liberate down the steep slopes of nearby Mount Judah to see how far they'd bounce and roll, and scheelite mines

TSS Earnslaw

There have been steamers on Lake Wakatipu since 1863. The twin-screw steamer *Earnslaw* entered service on the lake in 1912, the year the *Titanic* sank in the Atlantic on her maiden voyage. Like the *Titanic*, she was state of the art, with first- and second-class saloons lined with kauri and red beech timbers, and a sprightly service speed of thirteen knots (sixteen knots if pushed) that cut an hour off trips to the Head of the Lake. She was large, too, with capacity for 1,035 passengers. Tourism was taking off. The farming communities around the lake, however, were more interested in the space for farm produce — 1,500 sheep, seventy head of cattle, or 200 bales of wool.

The Earnslaw at Glenorchy. PHOTO COURTESY OF REAL JOURNEYS

In the 1950s, the steamship *Earnslaw* maintained a vital link with the outside world for the Head of the Lake settlements of Glenorchy and Kinloch. At Kinloch, passengers boarded the open-top buses for sightseeing and walking in the Routeburn Valley. The ship had an open bridge in those days. Glenorchy is in the distance.

The *Earnslaw* occasionally carried cars and buses to Glenorchy. This was before the opening of the road from Queenstown in 1962, which foreshadowed the end of her days on the Glenorchy run.

Built in Dunedin, railed to Kingston and erected there prior to launching, the *Earnslaw* has been dubbed 'The Lady of the Lake' in modern times. She is classified under the Historic Places Act. She puffs out historic smoke. Her one hundredth birthday celebrations in 2012 may see her sail again for Glenorchy if there is sufficient water at the wharf. The opening of the road from Queenstown in 1962, its tarsealing in the 1990s, and the encroachment of the gravel and sand delta from the Rees and Dart Rivers discharges, reducing water depths at the wharf, have combined to keep the *Earnslaw* out of the northern arm of the lake, more's the pity. The wharf has already been moved south once, by about 150 metres, to maintain a safe depth of water.

to explore. Back at his cousins' place, there were cows to milk.

The Lark's relatives lived on a farmlet. There were a few smallholdings around town. They had cows, which helped supply the village with milk, and sheep. They also ran stock on commonage land on the Rees River delta. It was rough pasture and free of charge. A few of the miners who owned stock and horses were allowed to graze them there. Over the years, however, the water table has lifted with gravel aggradation from floods, and the delta has become wetter, the pasture less productive.

Mining and farming — that was what made Glenorchy tick back then.

The 1950s Expression of economic prosperity in rural New Zealand was, 'a pound a pound'. It referred to the value of wool — £1 sterling for 1 lb of wool. These were boom years for sheep farmers. They were also pretty good times for miners of scheelite, another export that was worth £1 a lb for a while. Income from merino fine wool and scheelite made the Head of the Lake one of New Zealand's wealthiest districts per head of population, even though it had neither motor road access nor connection to the national electricity grid (it generated its own electricity from small hydro stations).

Glenorchy was the capital of scheelite mining in New Zealand. Mining in the hills above the town spanned the first eight decades of the twentieth century. There were frenetic peaks in production, and longer troughs, most of which were related to wars overseas — World Wars I and II, and the Korean War of the 1950s. Scheelite (calcium tungstate) is the ore of tungsten, whose steel-hardening properties are important for the manufacture of weapons, munitions and cutting tools. A heavy mineral and creamy (roughly the colour of the light patches on Simmental cattle), scheelite is mostly found in veins of quartz. Although the lodes around Glenorchy were patchy and unreliable, they did weigh in at seventy per cent tungsten content, the richest strike in New Zealand. If you were lucky, a scheelite 'lens' got wider the farther you blasted. But it was punishingly hard work, carried out in steep terrain. It involved pick-and-shovel digging, hammer-and-tap or jackhammer blasting with gelignite, and the laborious job of bagging. Then the bags had to be snigged out on an A-frame sled towed by a horse to reach a cableway connected to the stamper batteries for crushing.

These kinds of batteries were used in an earlier era for extracting gold,

Scheelite from steep places: a scene from the 1950s in the mountains near Glenorchy. Ben Gollop is working on the Bucklerburn cableway, which transported scheelite ore to the Mount Judah stamper battery. Looking after one of the mine horses, which hauled sledges loaded with sacks of ore to the cableway, is Glenorchy boy Desmond Smith.
PAT GOLLOP

although in this area more gold came from river gravels than from solid rock. Hundreds of miners rushed into the area in the early 1860s to get their share, which for the majority was negligible or merely a grubstake. As for hard-rock mining, the wonderfully named Invincible Mine was the most successful at winning gold from quartz. Traces of gold were often found with the scheelite ore through the twentieth century, and the precious specks would end up in a tobacco tin as a perk for the stamper battery operator. Glenorchy has Otago's most western cluster of gold workings; for the area is close to the edge of the schist and its lodes of gold-bearing quartz.

Not surprisingly, the scheelite miners downed tools in winter when snow covered everything. Even when the bulldozer replaced wheelbarrow, pick and shovel, and the overburden could be quickly stripped away, it was still a reasonably hard life, holed up in the clouds overnight, in small huts leaning at funny angles with the roofing iron held down by rocks slung from each side. Miners often slept with their clothes on. And it was no place to get injured. Ambulance or rescue helicopter services were unavailable in the 'fifties. Mining ranged almost to the summits of 2,000-metre peaks, and there were large scars all over the mountainsides. The notch on the side of Mount McIntosh close to the summit and visible today from Glenorchy, was created by scheelite miners.

Back in the 1930s, the Lark's uncle lost a mate in a rock fall. He was buried alive. The mining was all done privately then, and some of the scheelite ended up in Germany, ironically to aid the arming of the Third Reich. It wasn't till 1942 that the government bought out the main mining company, when the Western world, deeply into war by then, became hungry for tungsten. There were eighty registered miners at Glenorchy around this time, many of them exempted from war service for one reason or another, including being 'manpowered' for their mining expertise. Their main base was Campbelltown, a couple of kilometres up the road from Glenorchy, where there were rows of accommodation units for married and single men. Sports days in Glenorchy always featured strongman events such as caber tossing. Dances were held weekly in the local garage, the only suitable space.

When the Korean War broke out in 1950, the rising price for scheelite revived the mining, and Glenorchy boomed again. Between bouts on scheelite, a miner might turn his hand to an array of odd jobs. One man variously cut fence posts out of red beech, dug graves at the local cemetery, milked cows, cut hair and spread carrots 'buttered' with strychnine over tracts of land to kill rabbits for the Rabbit Board.

When it came to social life, the Mount Earnslaw Hotel was the hub. There was a piano for singing around and, in the 1950s publican Bob Stassen might crank up an accordion for his patrons' entertainment. Card games like forty-fives led to gambling and beer was swilled till the late hours, way beyond lawful closing time, on special occasions. There were two parts to the hotel: a twin-gabled main building, erected in 1880, and a two-storey guest room block with seventeen rooms, added in 1885. Guests had a good view of the lake 150 metres away. A public bar and a parlour bar, suitable for ladies, were in the original building.

Joseph Karley Birley built the hotel, one of three erected in Glenorchy in the 1880s to cater for increasing tourist interest in the Head of the Lake. The steamer *Jane Williams* (called the *Ben Lomond* after 1886) was in service by this time, bringing sightseers and mountaineers. From 1880, at the age of seventeen, Harry Birley, the proprietor's son, was guiding climbers into the Humboldt Mountains, and helping establish the Head of the Lake as a playground for the adventurous. The keenest, appearing thoroughly overdressed by today's standards in tweed jackets and hats, wanted to get as high as possible, and young Birley would lead them on ascents that included the paramount peak of the Humboldt Mountains, Mount Bonpland, 2,343 metres. Harry, in his mid-twenties, went on to become the first person to climb Mount Earnslaw — the East Peak — in March 1890. He climbed that day with photographer Frank Muir but having no ice axe, Frank had to stay at the foot of a steep wall of ice under the peak. Harry pushed on alone, reaching the summit in mid-afternoon. He left a shilling in a stone cairn as proof of his achievement, and three years later the 'bent shilling' was found by brothers Malcolm and Kenneth Ross where he said it would be, enclosed in a small bottle of Irish Moss cough mixture under the stones.

Fire was always a far bigger threat to the wooden hotels than raids by Queenstown police. After the Glenorchy Hotel burnt down in 1923, the Mount Earnslaw was left as the main centre of hospitality in town. But in the early hours of July 1959, it, too, succumbed to fire. The proprietor, his wife and their three children managed to escape just as the roof began to collapse. In thirty minutes, according to the report in the *Otago Daily Times*, the legendary hotel was 'a heap of crackling, burning debris'.

The Mount Earnslaw Hotel was the stage for characters of all kinds over the years — publicans, staff, patrons — none more memorable than Bill O'Leary, the Arawata Bill of legend, who based himself at the hotel in the early 1940s at the invitation of proprietors Stan and Kath Knowles. He wasn't the stereotype pub dweller at all. He was abstemious with alcohol, never smoked, and never swore. 'By Christmas!' was probably his strongest expletive. It was a favourite expression of his when he got worked up about something, and was even adopted by some of his friends as a nickname.

Arawata Bill, then into his seventies, paid for his board and lodging at the

Mount Earnslaw Hotel by tending the vegetable garden, feeding hens and milking cows — a kindly old cowboy and rouseabout. On some afternoons, he would sit out the back of the hotel preparing vegetables for the evening meal and talk to fascinated children going home from school. This white-bearded old gentleman in a suit with pocket watch and chain, who related well to the kids, had roamed the wildest, loneliest country imaginable between Glenorchy and the West Coast, ever hopeful of striking gold and rubies in profitable quantity. Although his fossicking days were over by now, he renewed his miner's rights at every opportunity.

Bill O'Leary could turn his hand to just about any kind of rouseabout work, on the farm or in town, although he was more likely to be found on a sheep and cattle station round the Head of the Lake when he wasn't prospecting in wild places. Had the brushtail possum been the resource it is today, with a promising fur industry based on it, he might well have been involved in trapping possums at the Head of the Lake as well, to earn some cash for the next bout of fossicking in the hills.

Harvesting possum fur can be as hard a caper as prospecting for precious minerals. It's an effort to get to the resource, you have to take the bad weather with the good, be prepared to rough it, and pray that your back and knees stand up to the loads.

Among the possum hunters working the Glenorchy area in the 1970s and 1980s was David Sharpe. The Sharpes had been at the Head of the Lake for decades, mining and farming. The war memorial in the main street carries the name of one of them. David's grandparents, Ernie and Marion Sharpe, told him stories about how Bill O'Leary would visit them at their home at Cosy Dell in the Rees Valley. He'd turn up from time to time, occasionally for Christmas dinner.

'Grandma insisted on Arawata having a bath before he did anything else,' David recalls. 'He used to tell them, "I've found the mother lode, where the nuggets are like plums in a plum pudding!".' Bill would announce the discovery in a characteristic, upbeat lilt. The Sharpes knew their guest was having them on, and that Arawata Bill hadn't found anything of the kind. But it didn't matter. Gold was a passion with him; it was his passport to the hills.

In his possum hunting days, David Sharpe roamed the hills at the Head of the Lake and elsewhere, laying lines of cyanide to kill possums. A squirt of cyanide paste on a rock, dusted with flour and nutmeg grains to entice the animal, was a tried and trusted recipe. The best pelts — they had to be at least ten inches wide stretched out — were harvested in late winter. Possums are essentially forest dwellers but they are hardy and adaptable. They can live in mountain tussocklands and shrublands, even in high rainfall areas, and range above the snowline, using rock crevices as dens. David has seen them near the summit of Coronet Peak. Most possums live at lower altitudes, however, and the boundary between the forest and the grassy river flats adjacent to the Southern Alps is usually a happy hunting ground for possum fur collectors. Possums, despite their arboreal image, like to add grass to their diet of leaves, buds, flowers, fruit, fungi, insects, birds' eggs and chicks. The label 'opportunistic herbivore' has been revised in recent years to something more sinister following video evidence of possums raiding kiwi burrows and the nests of birds breeding on braided riverbeds.

In the Rees Valley, along the edge of the forest, David Sharpe expected to get 400 to 500 pelts over a winter. He also hunted possums in the scheelite country near Glenorchy. The wetter areas, like the Rees Valley, produced mostly black and grey fur.

In the last week of June 1985, David was in the Rees Valley following a poison line along the edge of the forest near where the Lennox Falls plummet from an alpine basin. It was getting on for the middle of a cold, dull day, with snow starting to fall. Walking along a grassy terrace close to Lennox Creek, he saw a bird run up the trunk of a large beech tree that had been upended in a windstorm. He had the bird in view for not more than ten seconds — the time it took for the bird to get to the far end of the log before jumping into the forest. It made no sound. His first impression was that it was a blackbird. Blackbirds were common enough in the lower parts of the forest. But this bird, 'about eight inches high', was larger than a blackbird, its legs were longer, and it ran in a most unusual way. It was striding. Blackbirds hop. Although clearly anxious to reach cover, it chose to run rather than fly. That made David stop and think about what he'd seen.

He reported the sighting to the Wildlife Service office in Queenstown, which in turn sent a written report to the head office in Wellington. The description 'closely fitted that of a kokako', said the report. 'Mr Sharpe is an experienced bushman, having spent a great deal of time in oppossum [sic] and commercial deer hunting. He was not aware that officers of the N.Z. Forest Service claim there are kokako in the same area.'

David also told the Wildlife Service that he heard 'a strange call' in the Rock Burn valley the previous winter — 'something like a bellbird with a harsh call at the end'.

Wanting to see if he had any more light to shed on these reports, I contacted David. He lives in a weatherboard bungalow in Arrowtown, a short walk from the shopping centre. Although there is a reserve pressing hard up against the back of the property, he is a world away from the wild and wet haunts he's known chasing possum and deer. These days he drives coaches for groups of visitors, mostly Asian, on tours around the South Island.

He knows I have come about his kōkako sighting, but first, he wants to tell me something else of avian interest, involving his father, Peter Sharpe. His father, he says, rediscovered rock wren in Fiordland. Rock wren are tiny alpine birds, found only above the tree line. They spend a lot of time scurrying around at ground level, therefore, and become targets for stoats and other predators.

'Have you heard the story?' David asks me in a gravelly voice.

'I haven't. How does it go?'

'Dad was a scheelite miner at Glenorchy, and when the government put together a scientific expedition to Caswell Sound in Fiordland in nineteen fifty, he and another miner, George Ross, were recruited to prospect for minerals there. They didn't find anything much in the way of scheelite or other minerals but Dad did come back saying he'd discovered rock wren near the tops.'

'Runs in the family, these rare-bird sightings,' I say.

David still has a clear memory of his kōkako sighting at Lennox Creek. The thing that struck him most about his fleeting view of it was that it was running away to escape his intrusion, not flying.

The conversation moves on to possums, how he would work the Rees Valley in winter then move over to the West Coast to continue the hunt for what the Coasters called 'kiwi tree bears' or 'monkeys'. Possums were said to be strictly vegetarian in those days. Their status as predators of birds had yet to be revealed, although the forest die-back caused by their browsing was beginning to alarm the nature conservation movement.

Thinking now of forest health and human health, I ask him about an ailment called 'birch itch', which seemed to affect people in the past who were close to the beech forest. Beech trees were often called 'birch' by those involved in the

Touch of Scotland

Glenorchy is named after the hilly area of Argyll, Scotland, where there are snow-fed rivers, including the river Orchy, and forests carpeted with moss. Many of the street names are also imported from this part of Scotland — Mull, Islay, Oban, Jura, Argyll.

The first Europeans to occupy the site were two shepherds hired by runholder William Gilbert Rees, a burly Welshman, who founded Queenstown. The shepherds, Alfred Duncan and George Simpson, built a simple sod hut thatched with grass in 1861 'opposite the mouth of the Rees River, where a large lagoon opened off the lake'. Inside were two bunks, a couple of logs for stools, a fireplace and a food box lined with tin to keep the rats at bay.

timber business. Bill O'Leary complained of 'birch itch', and would avoid camp sites where he thought he was exposed to it.

'Yes, Dad got it bad,' says David, 'with a rash up his arms. People said it came from the bark. Possums got it, too; you'd see them rubbing up against trees.' (Back in Dunedin, I ask a dermatologist if he has ever heard of anything called 'birch itch'. He says he hasn't but, in turn, asks a Hamilton colleague who specialises in dermatitis caused by contact with plants. Back comes the reply: New Zealand beech trees contain no known agents that would cause an itchy rash. It remains a mystery.)

In addition to possum hunting, which was seasonal anyway, David Sharpe had other part-time work. He needed the income because the industry was having its ups and downs. When anti-fur lobbyists in Europe and North America succeeded in undercutting the market for anything made of natural fur, unaware that possums in New Zealand were at plague proportions and destroying indigenous forest and wildlife, David thought it was time to get out of the business. By this time he had a gammy knee, and his left thumb was sore and turning arthritic from skinning too many possums.

Younger and fitter hunters were joining the possum trade by this time. Thor Davis was one.

Thor had worked as a chef in Auckland. He had also worked and travelled in Australia for a few years with his wife, Corrine, who was from Blenheim. After returning to New Zealand in the early 1990s, the couple went kayaking on Lake Wakatipu and decided the Head of the Lake area was where they'd like to live. They spent seven months on Pigeon Island/Wawahi Waka initially, eking out a living harvesting possum fur, trapping stoats for the Department of Conservation and doing warden duties at trampers' huts in the summer. They moved to Glenorchy in 1994 and Thor continued with his possuming till he developed a knee problem from carrying big loads. In the remoter locations, a hunter might choose to carry one hundred skins on his back at a time, and one hundred skins equates to about seventy kilograms.

The possuming technique was similar to David Sharpe's the decade before — cyanide laid out in lines marked with surveyor's cruise tape at intervals of about twenty metres. Cyanide kills instantly and the possum is not going to get more than a metre or two away from the place it ingested the poison. Thor would expect to kill over sixty possums on every line laid, double the number if the strike was really good.

In 1997, there was a price slump for possum skins. It prompted Thor and Corrine to go into business on their own account as manufacturers of possum fur products. Glenorchy Fur Products was born, and a shop sheathed in corrugated iron opened in the town's main street, near where the stone speed humps are. It had a backwoods look to it, inside and out. The shop displayed jackets and vests lined with possum fur, and Russian-style hats with ear flaps. Teddy bears and boot liners topped sales in the early years. There were novelties, too, like nipple warmers. Bedspreads caught on later, and much of the business was export and mail-order.

Adding a new retail dimension to the main street, the little red-brown possum fur shop in Glenorchy, ten years on, appears to be flourishing. It is turning more than a dollar — it's turning a pest animal into a commercial resource. William Mason, of Paradise, did not live long enough to see the possums he liberated into his beech forest in the late 1880s become a forest-devouring, bovine tuberculosis-carrying pest. All he had in mind was a trapper trade in fur for garments and other manufactured goods. No one knew then how devastating the Tasmanian and mainland Australian possums would become in a paradise containing few predators, parasites or diseases compared to their homeland.

'Lucky to last six months' was what people said to Tommy and Reta Thomson when they took over Earnslaw Station in 1947. Rabbits, not possums, were the issue. Rabbits were rampant across most properties at the Head of the Lake at that time. On Earnslaw Station there were so many warrens on the flat paddocks between the Rees River and Diamond Lake that ploughing them became a nightmare. The tractor would break through the riddled topsoil and heel over. The station made more out of selling rabbit skins than it did out of farming sheep.

The Thomsons regarded the prediction of failure as fighting talk. Tommy was relatively new to the Glenorchy area, having arrived during the Second World War as a mining engineer to work on boosting the scheelite production. Reta was the daughter of a long-established Head of the Lake farming family, the Groves. With the assistance of the local Rabbit Board, which Tommy helped set up, and with a few newcomers to the area pitching in, they set out to drastically reduce rabbit numbers. Post-war immigration had brought new people to inland Otago, which is why a Thomson daughter, Jill, came home from Glenorchy School speaking some funny words — Greek, in fact, taught to her by children whose parents were spreading poison under the rabbit control programme.

The reason I know a little of the farm's history is that I made an appointment to talk with Geoffrey Thomson, the son of Tommy and Reta, who supervises the running of the station now that his parents are retired. I wanted to know more about the station before I headed up the Earnslaw Burn for another rendezvous with the Lark at the rock shelter he'd spoken of a few months back. He'd sent me another message, with a time and date. Part of the valley is included in the station's pastoral leasehold land.

I meet Geoffrey at the farm headquarters on the flats below Lake Diamond. His parents now live in a newer house a short distance farther up the Paradise road. The first thing I notice is that the station's name is now 'Mount Earnslaw', which Geoffrey explains provides a stronger branding for the produce coming from it, the meat and wool. There is minimal sign of rabbits these days. To the north, Wanaka's tourist promotion people have done something similar, adding 'Lake' to the name of the town whenever it is promoted, to emphasise Wanaka's lakeside location. Lake and mountain: powerful words in marketing.

The owner's house at the Mount Earnslaw Station is an unpretentious dwelling that has seen busier times, and no doubt more attention on the garden. It is empty for periods because Geoffrey, a civil engineer, is partly based in Christchurch, and often flies himself down to the farm in a light plane. The station's day-to-day operation is in the hands of a farm manager who lives elsewhere on the property. We sit down to a cup of tea at the kitchen table and Geoffrey describes the extent of the farm. It includes the flat paddocks down to the Rees River, most of Mount Alfred, and areas of the Earnslaw Burn valley above the forest. He talks about the stock as well: the Perendale sheep, Angus cattle and red deer. The deer are descended from animals captured live from Mount Alfred by helicopters equipped with net guns a few decades ago.

'Are you into tourism at all?' I ask, knowing that tourist activities are allowing other high-country stations to diversify in the face of marginal prices for meat and wool.

'A little. There's a company doing half-day Land Rover tours that uses our place, and a bit of heli-hiking goes on as well. Our main role is to provide the spectacular setting, that's about all.'

Geoffrey came back to the family home and farm in 1976 after working for consulting engineers for a number of years (in the summer of 1965–66, as an engineering student, he worked on the construction of the tailrace tunnel for the Manapouri Hydro-electric Power Scheme between Deep Cove and Doubtful Sound). The late 1970s were the Muldoon years, when Prime Minister Robert Muldoon's government paid out farm development, fertiliser and stock subsidies that, in today's unsubsidised environment, appear ludicrously generous. Farm development was deemed to be the road to prosperity. All that changed in the 1980s with Rogernomics, deregulation, user pays and the abandonment of farm subsidies.

I know that my conversation with Geoffrey will inevitably turn to a high-country controversy called tenure review. It's an epoch-making or epoch-breaking process, depending on which side of the fence you stand, involving the government, its agents and advisers on one side of the fence — a 'hot wire' most of the time — and the runholders who lease Crown pastoral land on the other.

At stake is a land area across the South Island high country that is larger than a host of South Pacific island countries — 2.2 million hectares, divided into 300-odd runs. The process, started in the early 1990s, is voluntary, verbose and vexatious. Into the new century it appears to have lost much of its initial composure, when all the talk was 'win-win'. The idea then was that runholders would win by being able to freehold — and therefore further develop with fewer constraints — useful parts of their leasehold land; and the government and people of New Zealand would win through the reacquisition of former lease-hold deemed to be too valuable for nature conservation, landscape integrity and recreational use to stay in runholder hands. In the former category, picture modified land of meagre natural significance and relatively low altitude; in the latter category, mostly a case of unmodified land, chiefly higher-altitude rangelands. A simple division? Peaceful co-existence, with each side in some sort of high-country heaven? Far from it.

The farmer lobby claims the process has been hijacked by nature conservation and public access imperatives, and the divvying up has emasculated runs and threatened their viability. The loss of summer grazing at altitude is a recurrent theme. On the other hand, the nature conservation/ recreation lobby says too much leasehold land is being lost to farmer and developer interests. 'Land grab', 'rip-off' and 'lose-lose' are labels now hanging over the process.

Into this high-country spectator sport, the government has thrown a few curve balls, not the least an arm-twisting hike in rents for pastoral leasehold land, and a decision to exclude from tenure review an array of runs that over-look water — the Midas touch for property sales in recent times — in case these stations gain a windfall on their newly acquired real estate far greater than anything they could envisage out of Lotto.

Geoffrey Thomson is a well-known figure in high-country farming circles and he has had a lot to say about tenure review over the years. He is also an articulate advocate for high-country traditions, whose enduring images include sheep flowing off muscular mountainsides of tussock in an autumn muster ahead of the first snows of the year, images that are bound to make even city dwellers feel good about life.

Today he's really steamed up about how the government has gone from valuing and nurturing rangeland farming a few decades ago to ruthless and unrelenting antagonism going into the twenty-first century.

Thunder and lightning

'I've seen great boulders brought down by the concussion of the thunder. And I've seen the lightning strike. I've seen rain that came down in sheets, turning the rivers into raging torrents as you looked … I saw a lightning flash splinter a great beech and fling the pieces all over the place. You don't sleep under trees in that country during thunderstorms.'

C.H. (Harry) Fortune quoting Bill O'Leary, in an article entitled 'The Passing of Arawata Bill', *Wide World Magazine*, London, October 1948

'They're trying to drive us out. How else can you explain the tenure thing and other policies? Look at the latest round of rent increases — Mount Earnslaw's proposed rent increase is eight hundred per cent! And this comes in the wake of meat and wool prices that are so low they're marginal for keeping the property going.'

He pauses a moment, perhaps to contemplate a telling argument that affects him personally.

'In this kind of climate the sons and daughters of high-country runholders are frightened to take on farming. Then there's the access band-wagon — city people wanting to treat the high-country as their playground, as if they've been denied access for decades. They haven't. They've always had access, simply through asking.'

The tea cups have been drained for some time now, and I need to be getting on. Tomorrow, I tell Geoffrey, I'll be heading up the Earnslaw Burn to the rock shelter, assured of access to a valley much less travelled than the Routeburn. Kōkako country a while back.

Because it's old history, over thirty years old, I don't feel like raising the fact that Mount Earnslaw Station lost sixty per cent of its leasehold land to Mount Aspiring National Park in 1973. The Minister of Lands at the time, who was also responsible for national parks, saw no need for the Earnslaw Massif, the Forbes Mountains separating the Dart and Rees Valleys, and the upper part of the Earnslaw Burn Valley to stay within a pastoral lease. These chunks of land, over 9,000 hectares in all, were mostly permanent snow and glacier ice, and cold, bare rock that chamois running wild could happily negotiate but not sheep.

I'm not going to those heights tomorrow but I will be in a back-country setting. There are no huts up the Earnslaw Burn after Mount Earnslaw Station's musterers' hut was burnt down. No bridges, either, and no carefully-graded track with handrails at the drop-offs.

Kea. DEPARTMENT OF CONSERVATION

CHAPTER 4

Starlight Hotel

Wicked country, but there might be
Gold in it for all that.

Under the shoulder of a boulder
Or in the darkened gully,
Fit enough country for
A blanket and a billy
Where nothing stirred
Under the cold eye of the bird.

Denis Glover, from
Arawata Bill: A Sequence of Poems, 1953

The high-walled valley of the Earnslaw Burn feels like a sanctum. It's a little-visited place, and it points straight to the heart of the ice-bound Earnslaw Massif, the highest block of mountains in southern New Zealand after Aspiring/Tititea. The valley runs north-south, shaped like a wobbly tuning fork and open at its southern end, where the river rushes out of a gorge to find its destiny not in the Rees and Dart Rivers that wrap around Earnslaw/ Pikirakatahi, isolating its bulk from the Main Divide, but in Diamond Lake. From a secluded source, the Earnslaw Burn sings its own effervescent tune.

On a gloriously fine mid-March morning, a day nominated by the Lark some time ago, I turn off Paradise Road at the Earnslaw Burn bridge, and drive up to a grassy parking area close to the beech forest. Silvery logs from past floods litter the area. A weather forecast on the radio that morning described a high-pressure system straddling the country. It's the time of year, somewhere between late summer and the onset of autumn, when you'd expect settled weather. The announcer said he had never struck a forecast like it — fine weather from one end of New Zealand to the other; cloudless skies and warm temperatures. Driving here, I noticed that the willow trees on the Rees Valley floor were turning shades of yellow, perhaps prematurely adopting autumn apparel through the stress of an exceptionally dry summer.

I check through my overnight trek supplies. The pack is not especially heavy. I have a small flask of Scotch in case of a cold night under the stars. Crossing the river and its shockingly cold water is the first challenge, then with boots squelching, I climb through the forest on the left bank of the river.

Among the legendary names of the district, who, I wonder, ventured this way? Did Joseph Fenn, the multi-talented and socially-challenged founder of Arcadia explore the Earnslaw Burn, or his older relative and neighbour at Paradise, William Mason? Did they see or hear kōkako, the red-tailed, tūī-sized New Zealand thrush, piopio, or the superbly camouflaged night parrot, kākāpō? All three species were almost certainly living in forests not far from Paradise in the late nineteenth century. Did Bill O'Leary stray from his beloved Dart River track to fossick for gold in this valley? Poet Denis Glover, immortalising O'Leary in a sequence of poems titled *Arawata Bill*, captures the atmosphere of a sanctum well when he writes of how the door of the proverbial valley — meaning many a valley in this part of the country — 'swings shut behind'.

There is a marked trail, which is probably used more by deer and other animals than by people. No woodland stroll, it is less well defined than the Sugarloaf Pass track. There are places where you have to squeeze between rocks, shimmy around fallen beech trees and ooze through boggy bits that threaten to suck you into knee-deep mud. There are also some steps large enough to require handholds of root or branch. Moss-covered stumps loom out of the depths of the forest, suggesting century-old logging of the red beech. But who would go to such lengths for a supply of timber?

Bush birds, nowhere plentiful, begin to impress for their diversity: tomtit, rifleman, grey warbler, fantail, parakeet. And an occasional robin slips into view, hanging sideways on a coprosma bush or fussing among the fallen beech leaves. Oh, to be sitting in a clearing by the side of the track around 1980, with an outdoors man and his daughter, both out tramping, and glimpse a kōkako in the subcanopy. Among the avian voices filtering through the forest today, none comes anywhere near that of kōkako. But I do hear the call of kea, the mountain parrot, on the wing, and, distantly, a liquid gurgle that is probably its forest cousin, kākā. Kākā are largely confined to old-growth forest, for they need decaying trees to nest in, and the nectar, fruit and insects available from a mature forest. I give the birds ample opportunity to investigate my intrusion into their world by resting often on the moss and fern.

On the 1:50,000 topographical map, 'Earnslaw', the rock shelter rendezvous appears to be somewhere near the upper limit of forest. It's not much more than seven kilometres from the Paradise road on the map, but the intervening gullies, creeks, windfalls, and my tuning-in stops, not to mention the 500-metre gain in altitude, drag out the journey. Anyway, to rush through a forest, whether it's new to you or not, is somehow offensive to its natural rhythms. Can trees, among the planet's largest living things, much older than mammals, hear without ears, see without eyes?

Towards mid-afternoon, and nearing the tree line, I notice a character change in the forest, with silver beech more prominent now among the mountain beech (red beech ran out a long way back). Soon I am walking in semi-open shrubland and stunted forest. Turret Head, conspicuous from the Dart Valley but seldom seen from this side, is standing tall in the distance, its knobbly ramparts silhouetted in the afternoon sun, and Earnslaw's skirt of glacier ice, most of it in shade, is a reminder of the increasing altitude. Here, the Earnslaw Burn has lost its rough-and-tumble nature and much of its volume. Instead, it babbles across a wide bed of gravel, clear, blue-green and enjoying its last few hundred metres of relative serenity before plunging through the first of its forested gorges.

I'm reminded of a line from a poem by the Cuban patriot-poet, José Martí, 'The stream of the mountains pleases me more than the sea'. His poem was put to music and made popular in the 1960s through the song, *Guantanamera*. Besides its socialist connotations, it hints at the fascination of headwater streams, of journeys just begun, of water tracking through terrain where humans often cannot go. The upper reaches of the Earnslaw Burn would surely please a high-country angler whirling a barbed fly at these

The Earnslaw massif.

sparkling waters, trout or no trout. How ironic, that in the absence of rain, the river's flow will nonetheless be increasing through the day from ice melt, its source.

The edge of the forest is patchy, as if fires in the past have made inroads on the tree line. The vegetation here is a confused mosaic of beech trees, shrubland containing small-leaved olearia and hebe shrubs, the giant speargrass *Aciphylla scott-thomsonii*, and snow tussock grassland, their golden flowerheads glistening. I look across the river for sign of a rock shelter. I am no expert when it comes to rock bivvies. Is the Lark here yet? From which direction might he arrive? I wander on, with the valley broadening into a subalpine zone. The track, looking like an overgrown sheep track, is suddenly a lot flatter and inviting. There is nothing more exhilarating than a flat walk among mountains with running water for company.

Exploring a few minutes farther on, I come upon a cliff of layered schist and ledges to the right of the track — likely habitat for falcons because of the burn nearby. Water is cascading over one side of the cliff. At its foot is a low over-hang, sloping towards the river and offering shelter from northerly rains. It contains makeshift split-level accommodation, the kind of shelter I fancy a family of North American Indians might build for use on seasonal journeys. There are two sleeping berths lined with dry tussock grass, each berth made level by a low retaining wall of rocks. The upper berth is protected by a canvas awning, the only imported material in sight.

If the Earnslaw Burn were in flood from a northerly storm and too dangerous to cross, this would be a blessing for anyone without a tent. But the shelter I am seeking, according to the Earnslaw map, is on the opposite side of the river. I backtrack.

'Ahoy!' shouts a familiar, though disembodied, voice. It is coming from shaded forest and a dark line of cliffs downstream, on the other side. 'Get your feet wet! Walk a hundred yards!'

So I end the trek as I began it, wading through the river. Considering its icy source, the water feels remarkably warm, solar-heated through the riffles, and strangely nurturing, too. A river is a paradox. Fish it for ideas and you'll find a creative entity, a community of plant and animal life, and a life force that is cleansing, thirst-quenching and buoyantly hopeful. But fish it, too, for its dark side and you'll discover an awesome power, death and destruction. Māori have long regarded water/wai as sacred and supremely important to health. A proverb expresses it thus: *He huahua te kai? E, he wai te kai.* Are preserved birds the best food? No, water is!

Holding these thoughts, I cross the Earnslaw Burn to be met by the Lark at one of his favourite haunts. Compared to the rock shelter on the other side of the river, this mapped one is a hotel. It has a lofty ceiling with beech trees overhanging it, beds and mattresses, a table fashioned from a flat slab of schist, a folding camp chair, a fireplace built of rocks, firewood stacked handy, and a water supply trickling off the overhang a short walk from the living space. There is even a new blue bucket, purchased for ninety-nine cents from the Warehouse according to the label, for collecting water. The rock ceiling is smudged from campfire smoke, and there is a wisp adding to it now because the Lark has a fire going with a blackened billy rigged up over it.

My first impression of the bivvy is that it is constructed of several huge blocks of schist that lean against each other and hopefully won't topple further — even in a major earthquake. Slabs of schist lying in the vicinity suggest it has been rattled in the past. The bivvy catches the morning sun but the afternoon sun reflecting off the brown face of the valley opposite, casts a strong diffuse light into it.

'Got a brew going. Gumboot okay?'

'Anything will do,' I say, dropping my pack and taking a seat on a smooth rock by the fireplace. I think about releasing my feet from the sodden socks and boots but they can wait. 'Nice place. When did you get here?'

'Late yesterday. Come over the saddle from Paradise.' He says this as if it were a Sunday afternoon romp instead of the crossing of a range steep on both sides. Forest swathes the Dart side of the range, tussock the Earnslaw Burn slopes, and there is a high-sided gravel pass at the top.

The Lark tosses another stick on the fire. 'Jack Holloway thought nothing of it,' he says, as if reading my sceptical mind.

'You mean the Otago climber?'

'The very same. Fit as a trout. He'd come up from Dunedin and stay at the old cottage on Arcadia, the one Joseph Fenn built for himself. He'd often have some of his varsity mates with him. For a bit of recreation — not the serious climbing he's famous for — he'd shoot over to the Alpine Club's Twenty-five Mile Hut in the Rees Valley. And what for? To pick raspberries, that's what. Could do it in a day, some people reckon — there and back.'

I haul out my map. This sounds like an incredible feat, and yes, I see it involves

Feeding habits

Unlike the North Island kōkako, which live mostly in podocarp forest, South Island kōkako tend to be found in beech forest. It is not a hard-and-fast rule, however. Stewart Island, undoubtedly one of the last refuges of the species, intriguingly has no beech forest so those birds had to be podocarp dwellers. And in parts of the West Coast, especially inland from Charleston, there have been reports since the millennium of kōkako calls and movements in the podocarp forest growing on limestone.

Although there are few records of their diet, it seems South Island kōkako eat a variety of forest products, including fruit (coprosma and horopito berries, for example), seeds, leaves, ferns, moss and insects such as beetles and caterpillars. Their stout finch-like bill, curved downwards, with the upper mandible overlapping the lower, would suggest a wide-ranging diet.

North Island kōkako feed like parrots, grasping the food item in one foot while perching and bending down to reach it. South Island kōkako may behave similarly.

Moss figures in the diet of both North and South Island birds, specifically the moss *Dicranoloma menziesii*, which forms on the ground and over logs, and can climb a short distance up trees. Typically the birds pluck 'powder puff' clumps off the moss with a sideways flick of beak and head, and searchers look out for the 'powder puffs' and the gouging into the soil as a sign of kōkako activity. The food value comes mainly from seed capsules on the stalks, which are stripped as the bird lifts its head. The moss is also a source of insects and water.

South Island kōkako. NEVILLE PEAT/COURTESY OF OTAGO MUSEUM

Fiordland National Parks in the 1930s. I knew he and his family holidayed at the Head of the Lake but I wasn't aware of the Fenn connection. Fenn died at Frankton Hospital in 1924, a few years before Jack Holloway's stellar spell of mountaineering.

'They reckon he'd break into a jog when the going was good,' says the Lark.

We sip our tea, with the roar of the river about twenty-five metres below the bivvy bouncing off the cliff face. I have read that in his sixties Bill O'Leary could also travel at a fast clip on his prospecting trips. The Lark is made of the same stuff. In the past I've been pushed to keep up with him.

'Hear any kōkako on the way in?' The question is not altogether tongue-in-cheek.

'Not a bong,' I say. 'Never really expected to hear anything.'

'Well, keep listening and keep looking.'

The Lark tells me he knows of a couple of deer hunters who were in the Greenstone Valley in the early 1990s and reported seeing a kōkako near the Sly Burn Hut, where the track turns off to the Mararoa River and Mavora Lakes. The hunters were from the North Island, and one of them was familiar with North Island kōkako. It was a reliable sighting. Much earlier, there were kōkako stories doing the rounds when the Lark was a lad holidaying at Glenorchy, including one about the shearer who shot a kōkako out the back of the Rees Valley Station woolshed around 1932, and other reports of kōkako, mainly calls heard intermittently in the Hunter Creek forest, the next major creek above the Lennox.

'Bird deserves its nickname,' says the Lark.

'Nickname?'

'The Grey Ghost. It's a spooky bird, too true. Cunning at concealment. Best chance of seeing a kōkako is before dawn, so I've heard. A ventriloquist, you know. Throws its voice real special like.'

I'm thinking it's a pity it hasn't thrown a few more feathers over the years. Only one feather that I know of has been recovered from the wild and scientifically identified. It came from Stewart Island in early 1987. Wildlife Service officer Dave Crouchley picked it up in the Rakeahua catchment — an area dubbed Koka Valley — during a joint Wildlife Service/Forest Service search over the 1986–87 summer. Presumed kōkako contacts at the time included the sighting of long-tailed bird flying with a slow wingbeat, and numerous calls presumed to be those of kōkako: 'took', 'clack' and a note 'like a guitar string being tuned'. Five kōkako were thought to be taking part in this contact, and the written report of it described the calls as having 'peculiar resonant and directional qualities' that made recording of them difficult. At the same time the valley's bellbirds and tūī were joining the vocal fray, 'noticeably excited'.

What of the feather? It was sent to Otago Museum zoologist John Darby with no hint of the possible source species. John analysed the body feather. It had a distinctive shaft structure and 'looseness'. He concluded it was from Callaeas. Nothing surer. For corroboration and molecular analysis, the feather was later passed to a researcher at the University of Amsterdam in Holland. Back came his assessment: Callaeas, yes, and from a living bird.

It's probably only of academic interest now, twenty years on, but no trace of this feather can be found. When the Dutch researcher left Amsterdam, the feather disappeared, adding international mystery to the story of New Zealand's most enigmatic bird.

No one has reported kōkako in the Earnslaw Burn for a long time.

Having had time to properly take in my surroundings, I am curious as to how a rock shelter so far off the beaten track should be so well appointed. My host tells me the beds were brought in for the use of a Department of Conservation gang who spent days clearing windfall trees from the track. The bed bases and mattresses came from the refurbished Dart Hut on the Rees-Dart tramping circuit. Those track-clearers certainly went to some trouble to get a good night's sleep. They mounted the wire-weave bases on to young beech trees cut to length and made level on a foundation of rocks. There are only three bed bases, but half a dozen mattresses to choose from, parked on their ends at the back of the bivvy. I notice, too, a bag of nails and another bag containing orange plastic triangles, hundreds of them, for track marking. Work in progress.

The Lark, I soon discover, has brought dinner. It's a rabbit from over Paradise way, freshly shot and skinned, and he sets it over the fire to roast.

'I like a roast of rabbit,' he says. 'Not the numbers there used to be, mind. RHD has knocked them back. That and the odd bit of shooting.' He is referring to the virus imported illegally years ago by southern New Zealand farmers desperate to control rabbit plagues.

While the Lark gets on with roasting the rabbit, I hang out damp socks and fetch water. The air is cooling down now but the rocks retain some heat from the morning sun. Central heating for half the night, as the Lark might say.

'Need to keep an eye on the socks,' I'm advised. 'A kea could make off with them.'

However unlikely that may seem, I am aware of the craftiness of kea. A writer friend of mine from Dunedin, Philip Temple, has a bundle of stories about their prankish behaviour and their intelligence. He has long studied kea in the field and written much about the parrot of the mountains. I relate for the Lark a story that Philip reckons best sums up kea intelligence.

Years ago, in the Crow Valley near Mount Rolleston, Arthur's Pass National Park, Philip was climbing high up on the valley's tussock slopes and came upon a group of kea playing around. He'd heard stories of the parrots picking the eyes out of dead climbers and wondered what they would do if he lay down and pretended to be dead or seriously injured. He stretched out on the tussock close to the track. Soon a bird came to investigate. He caught its movement out of almost-shut eyes. Then he felt a pebble land on his chest. The bird was flinging stones at him to see if the human really was dead. Philip threw the pebble back. In those days there was a sign at the Homer Hut in Fiordland, warning climbers to watch out for kea throwing rocks on them from a height.

The Lark's eyes lighten: 'Want to hear *my* best kea yarn? It's from the Rock Burn, not far from where we had lunch a couple of months back.'

Here then is the story. A kind of kea street theatre is what it's about. The setting, appropriately enough, is Theatre Flat in the upper reaches of the Rock Burn. The year is 1960, between Christmas and New Year. The Lark happens to be camped at the flat's rock shelter, enjoying a fine spell of weather and a break from his agricultural studies at Lincoln University. At the same time, closer to the river, three keen young trampers from Wellington, not much younger than him, are tenting at the edge of an open area. From their conversations he deduces they have just come over Park Pass after an arduous circuit through the Pyke and other valleys west of the divide, and they are heading for Sugarloaf Pass and the Routeburn road end next day, all going well.

The grassy area beside their camp site is picturesquely defined by huge boulders deposited by a glacier eons ago and a scatter of stunted beech trees, some of which, as if to demonstrate the dogged persistence of plant life, are sprouting right out of the boulders. It is a natural amphitheatre worthy of Middle Earth.

In the early evening, from about 6 o'clock, some twenty kea assemble at the site. It appears as if they have been summonsed. At least, that's how the campers and the Lark see it. What they see they can hardly believe. An older bird, looking rather sad and bedraggled, is in the middle of the clearing, encircled by the other birds. From the raucous chatter, the trampers conclude that the older bird is undergoing some kind of disciplinary action. A few of the encircling birds take turns at tormenting the accused, rushing at it and attacking it before rejoining the circle. After a time all the birds withdraw to roost on the boulders or in the trees, and later they reassemble for a repeat performance of their kea 'court'. The drama lasts no more than two hours, and all is quiet overnight. In the morning the birds have gone.

I tell the Lark we ought to drink to a yarn like that. I produce my whisky flask. The sun is low enough by now to justify a drink, although it is still illuminating the far side of the valley. This far west, the sun sets late. If nothing else the Scotch will ease the soreness in my feet.

'I never again saw keas behaving like they did at Theatre Flat that evening,' the Lark says. 'A Christmas treat, they were. Not as many keas around nowadays.'

The story reminds me of a BBC wildlife documentary, screened on television a couple of years ago, that compared animal intelligence across a range of species. Kea came out on top, beating even dogs. Colourful clowns, mischievous thieves, destructive scavengers or entertaining rogues, love 'em or hate 'em, kea have lived in these southern mountains for tens of thousands of years. Their population decline is a concern.

Meanwhile, we are dining on roast rabbit and a few trimmings that came in cans and the whole tasty caboodle is washed down with whisky. Not a bad combination. The Lark seems to agree. The Scotch has him talking.

'Last time I was through here, you know, I could have had venison for dinner. Come across a young red deer stag caught up in tussock. Strong as rope, snow tussock. The poor bugger's antlers were entangled. Had been for some time, judging by the way the ground was all gouged up around the animal. It must have got snagged while grazing underneath a clump of tussock. I took pity on it. Cut it free.'

We are silent for a bit, letting the crackle of the campfire and the rush of river water have their say. Whether the Lark is still thinking about the snagged deer, I'm not sure, but I'd be keen to hear his thoughts on an official form of entanglement that is exercising high-country minds big time. It is called tenure review — the great clash of pastoralism, nature conservation and outdoor recreation that looks like it will keep the high country embroiled in controversy well into the twenty-first century. I mention the pessimism I found at Mount Earnslaw Station and await my friend's response. It is not long coming.

'The old way of farming these hills is under threat all right,' he says. 'Formula's wrong, and the parties need to have a brew — sit down and review the whole thing. There's too much land going to freehold, and too much to DOC.'

He is chomping on a leg of rabbit now. 'Thank god RHD didn't do away with the bunnies altogether.'

'So what's to be done about the pastoral lease land?'

'It's downright unnatural to have hard-and-fast lines drawn through properties the way they're doing — the high bit to DOC, the low bit to the farmer. Nature doesn't work that way. Farming doesn't either.'

The Lark's approach to tenure review, although he admits to a vested interest through the mustering and fence maintenance jobs he lands from time to time, is to take representative parcels of land with the highest natural value out of pastoral lease but let sheep graze to fairly high altitude under grazing regimes geared to minimise impact on soils and native plant cover. Conservative grazing can benefit the natural values in tussocklands, he says — containing the spread of exotic grasses and keeping the invasive European broom and at least one kind of heiracium in check. Broom is a legume, like peas and beans, and sheep go for broom seedlings as if they were bean sprouts in a grass salad.

'Guess I'm talking sustainability here. It's about keeping the fine-wool business going — and the natural values — through grazing licences and manage-ment plans. It's not rocket science. But getting it established across two million hectares of pastoral lease land, well, yeah, that's bound to be a challenge.'

The Lark is not keen on the mass freeholding of land. He thinks if farmers were allowed to diversify land use under different lease and management agreements, there wouldn't be the scramble to freehold and cash up. He says that's when foreign capital is liable to rush in — the 'Mammon worshippers' (he reckons it's a wonder there isn't a peak around here named after the Greek

God of Riches) — and as a result of the influx of foreign money and personal values, the traditional high-country runholding culture gets whittled away.

'Bet your boots, there'll be mustering for some time yet, though. Know how to tell the dogs and the men apart come dinner time? The men are the ones eating spuds with their mutton. Hey, you want to talk to the Rees Valley Station folk about the future of farming up this way. I hear Iris Scott has some good ideas.'

I say I'll do that some time soon. I'd like to see the Temple Peak Station family, too, the Hasselmans.

We've drained the flask of Scotch. The sun's down and the first stars are peeping through the crystalline atmosphere. It's time to turn in. What a treat to have a mattress under the sleeping bag. Is there a pillow menu, by any chance? Someone has placed candlestick holders by the beds. This really is a five-star rock biv.

A cream-cheese moon, all but full, climbs above the skyline like a giant, newly released weather balloon, dimming the stars, pouring light into the bivvy and creating sharp shadows. There is no sound save the rumbling voice of the river, and in this setting it is certainly pleasing me more than the sea. Moonlight keeps the bivvy illuminated till some time past midnight, when the air, stirred by the river, grows distinctly chill. I am a light sleeper and waken a couple of times, each time to see stars in astonishing abundance, some piercingly bright but most just stardust. How many suns roughly the size of ours are orbited by planets similar to ours, with sentient life that's also staring through the heavens? The constellation of Scorpion, the easiest of the animal shapes to identify in the night sky, is slowly arcing towards the roof of our shelter, head-first, with its body stretching towards a massive tail and its red heart, Antares, pulsing.

Kay-aaah! Kay-aaah!

The wake-up call, at 6.41, is unmistakably kea. I don't see the bird but the Lark, who is already up and fiddling around by the fireplace, says he saw it flying past.

'On its own,' he says. 'How sad is that for a tribal bird? Your socks are safe.'

By his standards I've probably slept in. The sun is soon bothersomely bright but its warmth makes me feel like a lizard — activated by solar power. In a small pot over the fire is the Lark's breakfast staple. It's being stirred appreciatively. His oatmeal porridge, I notice, comes with a few colourful additives. He throws in a handful or two of pumpkin seeds, sunflower seeds and tiny brown teardrops of linseed.

'Any sweetener?'

'Honey,' he says. 'When I have some. I help a beekeeper mate over in the Rees with his hives. It packs a punch, does honey. They reckon it takes the nectar from five million flowers to make a pint of honey. That's what I call concentrated flower power.'

Arawata Bill, I have read, lived on porridge. Sometimes, on long expeditions, he would have it morning, noon and night when other food was scarce, or tucker supplies low, or the weather so bad he couldn't light a fire to cook up something he'd shot. He would make up a big mixture, sweetened with treacle or sugar, in a three-legged camp oven, eat his fill for breakfast and pack the remainder carefully as the basis of meals later in the day and the day after. He did not mind eating the porridge cold. It saved lighting a fire. In the camp oven he might also cook rice, beans and split peas. That oven was probably his most valuable possession after his packhorse.

Kākāpō clue

During the hunt for the critically endangered kākāpō in the wilds of Fiordland years ago, searchers knew the big parrot was somewhere handy when they discovered kākāpō feathers in rock wren nests.

The Lark, also used to living simply, is dressed lightly this morning — sans Swanndri. I take this to mean a fine-day forecast. His porridge is nourishing. We slosh milk over it, the milk powder having been whipped with water from the rock biv's fairy falls. The porridge, the aroma of a beech-wood fire and the sound of the river washing boulders smooth all speak of refreshment. There's no chance of a whisky hangover lingering for long. Yet conversation takes a while to warm up.

'Back to Paradise today?' I ask.

'Yep. Bit of willow to saw for firewood.'

'Will you spend the winter here?'

'Not sure. Got invites from the Strath Taieri. Winter jobs, nothing strenuous. Winter's mainly for loafing anyway.'

I try another tack. I've heard of plans for a ten kilometre tunnel to Milford through the mountains between the Head of the Lake and the Hollyford Valley. Described by the developers as potentially 'the largest New Zealand tourism investment in decades', it would markedly shorten the distance by road between Queenstown and Milford and speed up the flow of tourists. Instead of falling asleep on the return trip as they counted the sheep on the long loop around the Northern Southland plains, the bus-borne travellers would be asleep as they sped through Glenorchy on their way back to their Queenstown hotel. Queenstown tourism interests are right behind the ten kilometre tunnel project. Around Glenorchy, however, it's caused a ruckus. At Mount Earnslaw Station Geoffrey Thomson told me the idea was a serious mistake, economically and technically. He reckons it would be hard to make it pay — there'd have to be a big toll. And being nearly ten times longer than the Homer Tunnel, ventilation would be a major technical challenge even if the coaches were hybrid models running on electric power through the tunnel rather than diesel on either side of it. Geoffrey ought to know. He worked on the construction of the Manapouri tailrace tunnel, which is a similar length.

Between spoonfuls of porridge, I say: 'What do you think about this Milford tunnel business?'

Whether the Lark has just had a honey kick from the porridge, I'm not sure. His response is certainly energetic.

'Bloody terrible idea! We had the monorail years ago, then the blinkin' gondola up the Caples. Now, a tunnel! Okay, maybe it could be done and maybe tourist wealth would pay for it. But it would be the end of Glenorchy's special character.'

'How's that?'

'Glenorchy would turn into a pie-stop and toilet-stop, 'cept the tourists wouldn't stop. Too close to Queenstown. The buses would whiz through, hellbent on making the hotel for pre-dinner drinks.'

A mood of sullen reflection comes over the Lark. He says the whole attraction of Glenorchy, for him and a lot of other people, is its location near the end of the road.

'Me, I'd be looking for another backwater.'

For the sake of a decent argument, I put the developer 'spin' — half the travel time to Milford, giving a reduced carbon footprint. Plus less congestion at Milford around lunchtime. But my friend is having none of it.

'They don't make places like the Head of the Lake any more,' he says. That kind of punch line is a conversation-stopper. I take the hint. The here-and-now is pressing claims. Somewhere among the trees overhanging the rock shelter a grey warbler releases its wavering call, distinct from the river's deep voice, and I look around for sign of rain clouds. The sky remains clear.

'Hey, speaking of backwaters,' says the Lark, 'how are my surfing mates at Taieri Mouth?' He is talking about sea lions.

'I wouldn't recognise your mate Brutus from all the other males', I reply. 'But Mum's still around. Produced a pup at twenty years of age, even though her eyesight's going. She's a legend.'

The Lark tells me he keeps his Pirouette kayak in the Rees River area these days — the kayak he used surfing at Taieri Mouth — and occasionally goes for a paddle in its rapids when he can arrange transport.

It's time to pack up. The housekeeping is simple. A little fairy falls water extinguishes the fire and we restock the kindling for the next patrons of this starlight hotel. The mattresses are stacked upright to protect them from possum and rat excreta. The Lark will be heading back to the Paradise area by the route he came whereas I'll backtrack down the valley to my car and drive home.

'You can't go without seeing Earnslaw full-frontal. It's just around the corner.'

We walk up the valley along hare or deer tracks, aware of an autumn nip in the air. The river water, chilled overnight, is a shock to the feet. When the upper valley formed part of Mount Earnslaw Station, stock used to graze here. The introduced grasses grow rank now, suppressing the native species. The stock have long since gone.

We pass the small rock shelter on the river's left bank, a squeeze compared to the high-rise guest house across the river. After twenty more minutes of walking the grassy flats, the Earnslaw Massif/Pikirakatahi and the full sweep of the Earnslaw Glacier are exposed — mountain morning glory, rising almost two kilometres from the valley floor. Earnslaw's twin peaks are separated by over a kilometre of summit ridge, a thin white line. West Peak is on the left. East Peak, although ten metres higher at 2,830 metres, is the easier to climb. Wrinkled with crevasses, glacier ice grips the curving head wall of this cirque basin, and like many glaciers in southern New Zealand is only just holding on. The glacier once rode high, wide and handsome over where we are standing and joined the great Dart and Rees Glaciers in the last ice age.

As cul-de-sacs go, this place is more than emphatic. It is humbling. You can feel some sort of engagement going on here between the terrestrial and the celestial. A cirque of this scale and architecture is not so much a barrier to westward progress as an arena for the imagination. I have an inkling now why the Lark has chosen to commune with mountains rather than the sea coast, the source of 'ocean emotion', and why he has invited me here. The spirits lift, and not just because the sun is up and the sky a spotless blue shield.

From a shrubby patch nearby comes a short sharp squeak — 'seet, seet'.

'Rock wren?' I say, suddenly alert to the possibility of seeing something rare.

'Nope. Tomtit. You need to go higher for rock wren. But they're here all right, and ahead of us, at the foot of the glacier, is rock wren city.'

It's hard to believe such a dainty warm-blooded creature with matchsticks for legs — shorter than the robin's and giving the little bird a leggy look — could survive in this potent swirl of elemental forces: ice, snow, rock and occasional tempest. Rock wrens live their entire lives above the tree line. Even kea, characteristically alpine, will venture into forest, and in Fiordland sometimes descend to sea level. But the rock wren knows nothing of tall forest. Its home is in the boulder fields and patches of alpine shrubland, covered by snow for much of winter and spring.

Tuke

Most bird books do not record a Māori name for the rock wren. Nonetheless, southern Māori overlanders would surely have encountered the bird and given it a name.

Tuke (elbow) is said to be the name Waitaha people of the south applied to the rock wren in pre-European times, a reference to the bird's elbow-shaped eye stripe. Another name suggested for the species is tatarihuka (expect snow), which refers to a belief that if you killed a rock wren a snowfall would result.

Intrigued in the past by the survival strategies of rock wren, I've turned to Dunedin biologist Sue Michelsen-Heath from time to time for information. Sue has studied rock wrens since the early 1970s, when she first saw the bird in the Cascade Saddle area near the head of the Dart Valley and was immediately in awe of their ability to survive the alpine conditions. Actually, the species is much older than these mountains. With the rifleman, it belongs to an ancient New Zealand bird group comprising half a dozen species. Of the four extinct wren species, three were flightless — a very rare thing among songbirds. The last to go was the bush wren. It was last recorded in

Rock wren. C.R. Veitch, Department of Conservation

1972 on a remote small island off Stewart Island.

The rock wrens are thought to have evolved twenty-five million years ago. Just as kea and kākā separated into alpine and forest habitats, so too did the rock wren and rifleman go their separate ways. The fact rock wrens hatch chicks without down feathers while living in a harshly cold environment merely adds to the intrigue. Their nests are chunky pouches built of matted grasses, leaves, moss and feathers, with insulating walls six to eight centimetres thick and a tiny, heat-conserving entrance. Nests are found in gaps between rocks, under roots, in banks and sometimes in sheltered crevices on rock bluffs.

To survive the intense cold and heavy snowfalls, they hunker down in insulating nooks under vegetation or in rock crevices. How exactly they avoid freezing to death, being so slight, is difficult to explain. Active the year round, they do not hibernate like many warm-blooded northern hemisphere animals.

The Lark, observant mountain man that he is, is also familiar with the bird. He says he'll probably hear some wrens on the way back over the range. He may even see them. They feed on insects like moths and weta, and they comb coprosma bushes and snow totara for berries. They go for the nectar on mountain flax, too, and pluck tussock seeds.

They have a long hind claw for clinging to rocks. They are earthly birds, not given to flying far, with a strange habit of bobbing up and down on the spot and bowing with legs straight.

'They're into energy conservation in a big way,' says my friend. 'With their build, they'd be mad to fly any distance.'

'It's a damn quiet valley for birds,' I say. Apart from the warbler and tomtit we haven't heard a bird sound of any kind. 'Where are the paradise ducks and Canada geese?'

'Certainly not a birding day today. Stoats rule, even in remote places like this. They give the birds hell. Our forests are more fur than feathers these days.'

The morning is wearing on. We need to be going our different directions. It's agreed we'll meet again next summer, perhaps around the time of Glenorchy's renowned annual Race Day, the first Saturday in January.

'See you then,' I say.

'Not if I spot you first.'

I know better than to ask the Lark about his future. He would no more submit to a fixed abode and phone number than Bill O'Leary or various other southern men of the hills down the years — loners perhaps but not hermits.

Crossing the Earnslaw Burn, a mountain brook rather than a river at this high point in the valley, the Lark starts angling back towards the saddle that gives access to Paradise, Arcadia Station and Diamond Lake. Meanwhile, I follow the animal trail back to the tree line. My friend quickly becomes small on the tussock-brown slopes drenched by the morning sun. But his movement is eye-catching. He is powering up the tussock face, perhaps not as fast as I remember him going up Smooth Cone in the Strath Taieri many years ago, but impressively quick for his age, and with no dog to spur him on.

Classic portrait: Bill O'Leary, in three-piece suit and thigh gumboots, and his packhorse, Dolly, at the start of a back-country expedition from the Head of the Lake. This 1938 photograph by Thelma Kent is the best-known portrait of the legendary prospector.

CHAPTER 5

Going West

Human geography aficionados might care to take note: a road-end in a frontier land like the Head of Lake Wakatipu, where settlement rubs shoulders with a mountain fastness, is bound to contain more than its share of larger-than-life characters. They stand out not only because they are resourceful, self-reliant and skilled at many things, but also because their personalities leave a lasting impression. It is as if they have become deeply etched into the landscape. They seem to 'wear' the land, as the Lark would say.

Bill O'Leary wore the land. He also wore a three-piece suit, with fob watch in the waistcoat pocket, and thigh gumboots. A late 1930s photograph of him by Christchurch photographer Thelma Kent portrayed him dressed this way. He is standing by his beloved, big-footed packhorse Dolly, a seventy-year-old man with a snow-white beard setting out from Elfin Bay for the wilds of the Olivine country west of the Main Divide. Piled on Dolly are sacks stuffed with provisions for a three-month expedition. He has a wide-brimmed hat to protect his bald head from sun and rain, and the gumboots are reinforced with leather soles and hobnails for negotiating slippery stream beds and gripping steep terrain. It is the portrait of a legend of the south: Arawata Bill.

Although his nickname acknowledges one of the great rivers and valleys of South Westland, where he worked as a ferryman, roadman and cattle musterer, Bill O'Leary strongly identified with the Head of Lake Wakatipu. Off and on, over a period of forty-odd years starting in the late 1890s, he sought treasure in far mountains but repeatedly came back to the Glenorchy district to work for his keep and the cost of restocking the next expedition. Of wiry, athletic build, he could carry a pack of over twenty kilograms into the hills.

William James O'Leary was born on 28 October 1865 at Wetherstons, a goldfield near Lawrence in Central Otago. He was the second oldest of eight children of Timothy and Mary O'Leary (actually, Bill's mum and dad were married at Milton by a Scottish ancestor of mine, Alexander Ayson, a pioneer South Otago teacher). Young Bill grew up in a goldmining environment, and carried a gold-fossicking interest into the mountains and valleys out west. He was fit enough even into his seventies to be roaming largely trackless country. To mark passes and trails through high places he would erect piles of stones. In his seventy-eighth year, however, Arawata Bill appeared to Glenorchy friends to be ailing, and they arranged for him to go to a Catholic old people's home in Dunedin. For a while he appreciated the care and attention he received from the Little Sisters of the Poor in Andersons Bay but longed for the outdoors and had periods back in Glenorchy and Wellington, where his sister lived. He died in Dunedin on 8 November 1947, aged eighty-two. The legend wasn't laid to rest, however. O'Leary Pass, a saddle in the Barrier Range between the Dart Valley and a tributary of the Arawhata, commemorates Arawata Bill.

Quite a few characterful contemporaries of Arawata Bill loom large in the history of the Head of the Lake. They include Joseph Fenn, of Arcadia, Granny (Jane) Aitken, of the property next door, Paradise, and Harry Birley, mountaineer and mountain guide.

Like Bill O'Leary, Fenn was content with his own company, appreciated nature and the outdoors, and left few writings for posterity to judge him by. But unlike O'Leary, Fenn did have a permanent home in the Head of the Lake district, which he rarely left, and he built Arcadia House for visitors to admire a hundred years on. Born in the small rural English town of Stotfold, Bedfordshire, in 1854, he was the second oldest of five children, and the oldest son, of Joseph and Mary Fenn. The second-born took his father's name and his uncle's middle name as well. His uncle, Christopher Cyprian Fenn, had an illustrious thirty-year career in charge of the Christian Missionary Society. The family had its own coat-of-arms.

When Fenn was just sixteen, his mother died. She was forty-seven. Family-tree records note dryly that he emigrated to New Zealand about 1880 'following disagreement with father' (this, of course, is the father who is alleged to have moved in on his son's fiancée following the mother's death). That his

Arcadia House: a 1970s drawing. Audrey Bascand in *Old Buildings of the Lakes District* by Marion Borrell, published by David Johnston. Reproduced with permission of the artist.

father married again is recorded in the family tree, as is the birth of a half-brother, Bernard Samuel Fenn, in 1875, when Fenn snr was aged fifty-five and his second wife twenty-eight. On the surface of it, the twenty-seven year difference between his father and stepmother is fuel for the fiancée story. But the marriage occurred in 1873, when the oldest son was around nineteen years old. Given a seven year age gap between Joseph and his father's second wife, the possibility of Joseph Fenn jnr having had a prior relationship with her becomes somewhat remote. There were about three years between his mother's death and the remarriage of his father — time enough, I suppose, for some trouble with a fiancée but not necessarily his future stepmother. The family tree also bluntly notes that Fenn, newly settled in New Zealand, was 'Not a remittance man'. Presumably, then, he arrived with sufficient funds in the bank to start a future life on the other side of the world, and a long way out west, as a landowner, farmer and the builder of the Head of the Lake's most striking house.

All this discussion of family ties is mere skirting around the character of one of the district's deepest personal mysteries. Joseph Fenn, 'sheep farmer, of Paradise', kept more or less to himself and his property for all but a day or two of the forty-four years he spent in New Zealand.

After he died in January 1924, the *Lake Wakatip Mail* carried an obituary, written by an unnamed Glenorchy correspondent, that heaped praise on him for his 'strong character', 'sterling worth', and 'generous nature'. He was described as 'very sensitive and reserved'. He 'never took part in public affairs' but if approached to donate to a charitable cause, said the obituary writer, he would happily contribute. He never married and had no known relatives in New Zealand apart from his aunt, Kate, second wife of William Mason. He had a 'stainless life', the obituary affirmed. Moreover, he 'loved nature and the simple life'. Pity those last words do not figure on his headstone.

He died in the hospital at Frankton of 'cancer of the liver, jaundice, heart failure', according to the death certificate. It was a quiet funeral. He was buried in a plot near the upper edge of Queenstown Cemetery, about as close to a forest (Douglas fir in this case) as was his cottage to beech forest at Paradise. The headstone is a black column mounted on a plinth that carries the name F E N N, with a coat-of-arms-like floral graphics wrapping around the gabled top of the column. The inscription, newly repainted in silver (by whom?) when I visited the grave in 2008, reads:

Joseph Cyprian
FENN
DIED
3rd January
1924.

Fenn does have an epitaph in mapped form, however — a group of Greek mythological names on several peaks at the northern end of the Humboldt Mountains: Poseidon, Chaos, Amphion, Niobe, Minos. He is credited with applying these names, consistent with the theme initiated by surveyor James McKerrow.

The year Joseph Fenn died, another Head of the Lake personality, a home-grown one, passed away. Harry Birley, first person to climb Mount Earnslaw

Fenn's cottage.

Mt Earnslaw and Mt Alfred (left).

(1890), was one of the district's most celebrated mountain guides. The son of the Mount Earnslaw Hotel's first proprietor, he became an experienced climber while still a teenager, and led many guests of his parents' hotel to summits in the Humboldt Mountains and to Mount Earnslaw. Among them was an English botanist of international renown, Lilian Gibbs. Harry's interest in alpine flora led to the naming of a low-growing high-alpine shrub species after him — *Parahebe birleyi*. It lives in rocky terrain under snow much of the year, ranging to an altitude of almost 2,000 metres — very much Harry Birley country.

Unlike other Head of the Lake characters who arrived in the district as adults, Harry was raised here. He soon added 'postmaster' to his title of guide, and in World War I was a scheelite miner with a claim at 1,500 metres on Mt Alaska, above and beyond Mount Judah. He died at East Taieri near Dunedin in 1924, a couple of years after arriving there.

Another high-profile pioneer of the Head of the Lake visitor industry was Jane Aitken. She and husband David — and later some of their children — ran Paradise Guest House after the Masons had established it. From 1890 to 1942, Jane Aitken and her children were pillars of hospitality locally. Entries in the visitors' book testify to this.

Born in North Devon in 1859, Jane emigrated to Australia and New Zealand in 1876 as an adventurous seventeen-year-old. Attracted to Queenstown in the role of governess to a banking family, she met an immigrant gold miner from Fife in Scotland, David Aitken, and married him in 1879. They had six years at Skippers before moving to the Head of the Lake, where the Masons engaged them to run Paradise House. From 1893 they owned the property.

Jane Aitken's role as Paradise hostess spanned the years of horse-and-buggy (a two and a half hour trip from Glenorchy), the first automobile service in 1919 and finally, around 1940, the introduction of a convertible bus, similar to the tourist buses operated by the Bryant family between Kinloch and the Routeburn Valley.

Visitors to Paradise were always assured of hearty food, with Jane and later her daughter Isabella (Poppy) designing the menus. Breakfast would typically comprise porridge and trout caught in a set net in Diamond Lake and recovered around 6 a.m. by David Aitken, who rose early. Lunch was often cold roast lamb or venison, and the evening meal roast meat and home-grown vegetables in season. Bread mixture was mixed in two four-gallon kerosene tins and set by the warm stove overnight to rise. Being the proprietor of a popular guest house was hard work. The washing of linen, for example, was all done by hand.

During the Great Depression years of the early 1930s, following the death of David Aitken in 1928, 'Granny' Aitken took hospitality to new and selfless heights when she offered lodgings and food free of charge to miners struggling to make a living from extracting scheelite from the Paradise mine at the northern end of Mount Alfred. Paradise House struggled in turn. In 1932, the Aitkens were forced to sell Paradise to the Glenorchy storekeeper, Jack Thornton, to pay for debts run up at the store. But the family continued to manage the guest house business till 1942, when Isabella had a heart attack and died. Her mother lived till 1954.

In the tradition of Aitken, Fenn, O'Leary, Birley and others, Glenorchy remains a natural haven for characters, a destination for resourceful and make-do personalities who like the idea of living alongside a spectacular wilderness. In the 1990s, one man who'd studied Norse mythology at Oxford University and was a kind of horse whisperer, restocked the Department of Conservation trampers' huts for a few seasons, using coal-carrying packhorses roped together to form a train.

Imprint of an umu (earth oven) at the Dart Bridge camp site.

I have a theory as to why the Head of Lake Wakatipu is a gathering ground for characters. There are two parts to it. First, the district is a cul-de-sac, and road-ends anywhere tend to be character-forming. Second, it is a natural pathway west. That factor, as I shall explain, intensifies the pulling power of a place, especially when its setting is as spectacular as Glenorchy's. Glenorchy has pulling power in fairly full measure. Call it G-force.

Many countries and peoples involved in colonisation have a westering tradition. Consider the Vikings over a millennium ago and their movement west into the British Isles and Iceland, and earlier waves of settlers from mainland Europe who invaded Britain and Ireland. A popular traditional Scottish song, 'Westering Home', which I'm sure the Lark could whistle as he did 'Road to the Isles' back in the Strath Taieri, tells of homesick travellers in the Orient longing to return home. It tugs at the heartstrings. Consider, too, the experience of British colonisers in Australia. They settled eastern harbours before setting out to explore the interior of the desert continent all the way west. Then there is the United States, again settled by British emigrants on the eastern seaboard (although Native Americans migrated from Asia by way of a land bridge). The European Americans have the most compelling and dramatic tradition of westward exploration. West was where the promised lands lay. The westering tradition shaped a nation. It took the best part of 200 years for the West to be settled all the way to California. A whole industry was based on Western movies, including the 1962 epic, *How the West was Won*.

Rewarded for carrying water

Among Māori traditions is the story of how the kōkako got its long legs. When Maui, the man-god, became thirsty after an epic struggle to slow the sun's movement and win a longer day for people, he asked the birds of the forest to help him quench his thirst. The kōkako responded, filling its wattles with water for him. To reward this act of kindness, Maui lengthened the bird's legs so that it could move more quickly.

Westward Ho! is both an American term and the title of a 1935 movie starring the biggest — if not the most convincing — cowboy of all, John Wayne.

New Zealand, too, had a European settlement pattern that favoured the eastern seaboard in the first instance. This was especially so in the south, the broadest part of the South Island. The white settlers who developed farmland in the east did not seriously explore inland Otago and the southern lakes of Wakatipu, Wanaka and Hawea until 1853, five years after the first immigrant ships arrived. But once the so-called waste or empty lands were traversed and the first maps grew more accurate, there followed a rush of pastoral farmers westwards.

Not surprisingly, given the intervening rangelands and relative isolation, the westernmost valleys at the Head of Lake Wakatipu were among the last in Otago to be occupied by sheepmen and their merinos. With the discovery of gold came another wave of exploration and settlement westward.

The first European to reach the west coast from the Wakatipu region was an Irish gold prospector and miner, Patrick Quirk Caples (his middle name was his mother's maiden name). In January 1863, alone and without either map or gun, he followed an old Māori trail up the Routeburn/Te Komana and over the Harris Saddle/Tarahaka Whakatipu to the Hollyford Valley and Martins Bay. At the time there were stories doing the rounds of the need for prospectors venturing west to look out for ferocious Māori and their formidable taniwha, not to mention giant moa. These warnings did not put Caples off but he travelled warily. Besides the Route Burn, which he named, he also found the Greenstone Valley route to the Hollyford. From Caples' explorations came a string of place names, among them Lake Harris, Caples Valley, Hollyford Valley and Hollyford River — Hollyford being Caples' home village in County Tipperary, Ireland. Official parties led by James McKerrow and explorer-geologist James Hector were also active in the region the same year.

In February 1863, Hector had instructions from the Otago authorities to investigate the establishment of a western port and settlement for the province at Martins Bay on the South Westland coast. He went by sea, aware of the menacing uncertainties of overland travel. In Dunedin, the idea of a port on the region's western seaboard — and views of the sun setting over ocean — no doubt appeared promising but as Hector and other pathfinders discovered, the Lower Hollyford River at Martins Bay had a bar across its mouth that was constantly shifting. It wasn't long before it was pronounced a hazard to shipping. The second boat carrying settlers was wrecked on the sandspit. Moreover, this coast, where South Westland meets Fiordland, was a weather coast, exposed to storms and high rainfall. Shipwrecks, isolation, a wet climate and poor soils for agriculture eventually put paid to the vaunted Martins Bay/ Jamestown settlement.

On his reconnaissance visit to Martins Bay, Hector was accompanied by Māori guides who showed him the known pathways east to the Wakatipu catchment. With this information and that of unofficial explorers like Caples, a road was envisaged but never realised. The demand for it simply petered out. The South Westland coast was no California. But for the inhabitants of the south who preceded the European settlers and whose villages were on the east coast and overlooking Foveaux Strait, the Head of Wakatipu was a western destination of immense value.

They came in the late spring and summer, wearing rain capes made from the waterproof leaves of tikumu, which was one of the celmisia mountain daisies, or harakeke/flax. On their feet were sandals woven from tough tī/cabbage-tree fronds and gaiters of the same manufacture to protect their legs from the stabbing golden spear-grass and other prickly vegetation. They literally wore the land's resources, and they lived off the land, too, harvesting tuna/eel, pārera/grey duck, and stems of tī kouka/cabbage tree as they travelled. They named an array of peaks, passes, rivers, streams, lakes, islands, resting places and camp sites at the Head of Lake Wakatipu. Within twenty kilometres of Glenorchy, whose first name was Tahuna (beach), there are thirty known archaeological sites. These early southern people explored widely.

Although there is little to see on the ground these days apart from a series of grassed-over pits, their camp seven kilometres up Te Awa Whakatipu/Dart River, on the right bank and close to the present-day Dart Bridge, is a window on their lifestyle, diet and handcraft. It is a moa-hunters' camp with a view of Oturu/Mount Alfred, Turret Head and, most significant of all, the distant peaks to the north, called Te Koroka, which McKerrow named the Cosmos Peaks. The choicest cuts and leg joints of moa were cooked in umu/ground ovens heated by pre-fired stones. Requiring slower baking, in the order of forty-eight hours, were the stems of young tī, which converted the starch to sugar. The product was a sweet energy-rich syrup that was as thick as toffee when it cooled. Another source of carbohydrate was aruhe/bracken fern, although its roots were conspicuously tough on teeth.

Eel were caught in specially-designed traps, gutted and hung out to dry on a frame of saplings. The preserved tuna was carried on forays farther west or on the journey back to coastal settlements. Archaeologists have identified from the kitchen middens, where bones were discarded, birds such as kākā, tūī and pūteketeke/crested grebe. No doubt the hunters also hoped to spear or snare kukupā/New Zealand pigeon and koreke/New Zealand quail.

For shelter at this seasonal encampment they built huts of rounded construction with thatched roofs, and laid branches against the tussock thatching to secure it in northwest gales. The dwellings lacked foundations but there were pathways of flat stones leading to the doorways, sometimes in a mysterious meandering fashion that has had archaeologists debating their purpose.

Local food and fibre resources guaranteed survival so far from home — an estimated eight days' solid march from the nearest (southern) coast — but the main object of these expeditions was stone, one particular kind of stone. A rare form of pounamu/greenstone was found in the mountains overlooking the Dart River and Routeburn. It was called inanga or inaka, a pearly-white or pale green-grey form of nephrite, named after the semi-transparent whitebait that migrated from the sea and was netted in the lowland rivers in spring. It is formed from twisted and tangled crystals that appear felted under a microscope.

At some point in their exploration of the Head of Lake Wakatipu and Te Awa Whakatipu, a party of Waitaha moa-hunting people from southern New Zealand came across the inaka deposits. In addition to the Slip Stream source, similar stone was found in the lower Routeburn/Te Komama area. Stone from this latter source was subjected to an unusual firing process.

The Dart Bridge camp site is more than 400 years old, and appears to have been occupied for two periods, each about one hundred years long, the earlier period dating back as far as 700 or 800 years. It is hard to say when the Slip Stream deposit of inaka was discovered but the prospecting ability and stamina of these early travellers is beyond question. They were a rugged, determined people, and they returned to the coast with news of a momentous find in a valley that lay below the face of a giant they called Te Koroka, which can be seen from the Rees-Dart track.

Strictly protected as a Special Area today under national park regulations (entry with written permission only), Slip Stream contains a major strike of the inaka form of pounamu, which is managed for the benefit of local iwi. There's a quarry under a crumbling cliff where people extracted portable pieces in the past, some of which were broken down by boulders dropped from a height.

The moa-hunter camp beside the Dart River. Chris Gaskin/Department of Conservation, Dunedin

It appears the people here used backpacks of plaited flax to carry their precious stone out to the river-bank camp downstream on the Dart, and to other manufacturing sites. Raw pieces of it found naturally in the bed of a stream seemed to shimmer as if alive.

In 1971, a Southland Museum expedition investigating a report from a commercial deer hunter came upon a massive boulder of inaka, about four metres long and estimated at over twenty tonnes, in the flood plain of Slip Stream. This boulder moves — an impression gained by iwi groups visiting Slip Stream from time to time. If there has been a flood since their last visit, the streambed may have shifted, creating the illusion of a mobile boulder.

Pounamu in any form is a taonga or treasure, and ownership of it is now legally vested in the South Island iwi, Ngai Tahu. It embodies mana — prestige, authority, high status. Among the most beautiful of minerals, it is astonishingly tough. Yet it warms to the touch. It was fashioned into weapons, tools and ornaments of exceptional beauty without the aid of metal tools, and its association with Māori culture carries beyond the utilitarian into art and mythology. Its inaka form, renowned for the quality of its translucence, is the reason the coastal people of old marched a long way west. Worked objects made from it have turned up in archaeological sites as far away as Northland.

Going west, therefore, figured strongly and at times dramatically in the story of early Māori and European travel and settlement in the south. There is something about the concept of westward travel that holds a fascination for me. Maybe a lot of people subconsciously feel the same way. How deeply rooted is this fascination? For Europeans, could it derive from a very ancient memory of migration west from the Caucasus and other regions of West Asia towards the setting sun? Travelling across Otago from my home on the east coast, I can feel buoyed by the prospect of following the sun for half a day and thereby gaining a few more minutes' extra daylight.

Early Māori trails took them all the way west to the sea coast; Pākehā followed the same trails but never developed them into motor roads. It wasn't for the want of trying, however. The Otago Provincial Council had grand plans for a horse-and-coach road through the mountains to Martins Bay in the nineteenth century, and in the twentieth century the impetus for a motor road west came mainly from Head of the Lake farmer and former mining engineer, Tommy

Thomson of Mount Earnslaw Station: father of Geoffrey Thomson.

For much of his life, Tommy Thomson has been a vocal proponent of a toll road west, following the Greenstone Valley and connecting to the Milford Sound highway near the Lower Hollyford Valley road intersection. There are cost and access issues. The road would have to cross national park land at the top end of the Greenstone. No stranger to roading development (he had a prominent role in the building of the Glenorchy-Queenstown road during his long role in local government, including sixteen years as the Lake County Council chairman), Tommy remains convinced of the value of a tolled Greenstone road, built on the other side of the river from the walking track to help separate trekkers and motorists. The new-fangled ideas of going west — a gondola up the Caples Valley and a road tunnel under the Humboldt Mountains — will not dissuade him. Why should it? Tommy turned ninety in 2007.

Farming, meanwhile, has met a road-block at the Head of the Lake. It has gone as far west as it will ever get. Nature stands in its way — a mountain bulwark, a wet climate, sodden soils. I'd like to meet some of these frontier farmers. No doubt there are characters among them.

Brink of extinction

'They [the South Island kōkako] probably died out on the South Island about 1960, and only a few, if any, remain on Stewart Island.'

Barrie Heather and Hugh Robertson
The Field Guide to the Birds of New Zealand, 1996

Rees Valley merinos, a hardy high-country breed.

CHAPTER 6

Blades and Traps

I am prepared to travel a long way west to see blade shearing, and do just that, at the invitation of Temple Peak Station's Mark Hasselman, on a crisp day in the middle of October. I admit to being a sucker for blade shearing. I like the concept, the simplicity of it, and the quiet, composed atmosphere, although, truth to tell, most of my experience of farming has been gleaned from television's *Country Calendar* documentaries.

Last time I saw a blade-shearing gang in action was on a sheep run called The Redan in the Strath Taieri near Middlemarch. The Lark was part of that scene, a smooth mover on the boards. I was taken by his flowing movement as he separated the fleece from the Romney ewes. His shears, on the long blow, were like scissors scything through paper — 'whisk-whisk, whisk-whisk' — and he spoke to the sheep as he carefully handled them.

After over four hours' driving non-stop, I reach Temple Peak Station, a short distance up the Rees Valley, about 11 o'clock in the morning. In a shearing day, this is roughly midway between smoko and lunch. Mark, known to his mates as 'Huss', told me over the phone there were 2,000 sheep to shear over three days — 1,000 wethers, 900 hoggets and a gang of rams, all merinos.

Outside the woolshed there are cars and utes parked at odd angles and a couple of farm dogs on chains, with chewed bones at their feet. The light from a powerful spring sun is embellished as it bounces off the new snow wrapping the upper half of the adjacent ranges, above the dark-green belt of beech forest. It is a bonny day. The mountains have never looked better. From inside the shed, which is a lot larger and newer than The Redan's one hundred-year-old wooden one, comes a steady beat. A portable stereo is pouring out music, dance strength. I enter, anticipating dim conditions typical of a woolshed. But the aluminium lining on the ceiling is reflecting a good amount of light, certainly enough for me to quickly take in the scene: eight shearers, in a line, their feet clad in moccasins, three female shed hands continuously on the move and Mark, who is at the end of the wool-handling line, classing the fleeces as they fall on his table.

'G'day,' he says, his lanolin-shiny hands feeling the next fleece and swinging it in the direction of a bale. 'Not a great place for conversation.' He's referring to the black ghetto-blaster at the far end of the shed.

'Yeah,' I return, voice raised, 'I thought blades were quiet.'

I can't hear them whisking at all. But the steady movement of the shearers' arms and hands I do remember well. Except that a few shearers are supported around the midriff by a padded stretchy harness they call a bungy, suspended from the rafters. As they lean into their work, the bungy, rather than their back muscles, takes some of the load.

'Hoggets today,' says Mark. 'Should get through the lot.'

One of the bungy shearers, in blue singlet and jeans with a knee torn out, looks familiar. He has roughly the build and ginger complexion of the Lark, with receding hairline. But he is not the Lark. He has a droopy moustache and a string of tattoos down both arms, featuring birds. An eagle is prominent, in braking flight, talons extended, and a swift is swooping. Or is it a swallow? He has good control of the sheep, which are being fleeced for the first time in their lives. As he despatches the shorn one and collects another from the pen, he shuffles with a stoop characteristic of a shearer who has been around many a shed — a back more stiff than sore and not worth straightening.

Mark points out the shearing gang boss, Ronny Hill, from Balclutha, and I go over to him to ask if it would be okay to take some photos. 'No problem.'

It's not possible to converse with a shearer. Talking expends energy, defeats concentration. All these people around you: but during a two-hour burst on the boards, you live in a lonely shell occupied only by you and a procession of sheep. In an eight-hour day, on hoggets, you hope to get through about 150.

The women rousies, meanwhile, collect the fleece as it falls free and carry

Mark Hasselman at the Temple Peak Station woolshed.

it to a table where they spread it and check it for imperfections — greasy bits, manuka seeds, hay and other embedded objects. They trim out the neck wool. Mark's job is to check the wool for fibre diameter and class it for quality, strength, colour and length.

'Merino hogget wool — finest of all,' he says, trying to compete with a rafter-rattling Jennifer Lopez pop song.

'What's it worth?'

'A bit under ten bucks a kilo these days. It hit twenty-five dollars in the heyday. That's nothing more than a memory now.'

Central Otago's dry rangelands have a reputation for top-value fine wool, and Mark confirms that merino farming on the Rees Valley hill country is affected by the rainfall.

He says the wetter the area, the lighter the fleece, and rainfall increases 'an inch a mile' the closer you get to the Main Divide. All in all, the lower prices for wool, the rainfall gradient and soil conditions make the Temple Peak property a tricky place in which to turn a profit.

At the lunch break, I approach Ronny, the shearing boss. He is tucking into a steaming plateful of beef stew, mashed potatoes and mixed vegies, prepared by Lulu, the gang's well-regarded cook. It's the kind of fuel you'd expect shearers to require midway through the day. After all, as an Otago University physical education study concluded some years ago, shearers expend the energy of joggers, and for eight hours a day. I ask Ronnie about the music. He shrugs the rounded shoulders of a body that spends most of its working day stooping, and says: 'It's a running argument. The shed hands like their own compilations, all modern stuff. You've got to keep them happy. The older shearers prefer a radio station but we can't always get that in the high country. We do a deal. Pop music flat out for an hour then we switch to radio for the next hour if we can get it, and alternate like that through the day.'

Ronny forks a few more mouthfuls thoughtfully. 'Shed hands have a lot more say than in the past. We value them.'

'And the guy in the blue singlet?'

'That's Jim — Jim Bool. Been around a fair while.'

I catch up with Jim in the sun outside the shed. He's from Timaru. His shearing career spans thirty years. He's shorn sheep all over the South Island high country with blades and machine shears, and he's a fan of the shearers' bungy, which was introduced a few years ago.

'A great idea,' he says. 'Takes thirty pounds' load off. Feels like you're floating. Over in Western Australia, a bungy's compulsory. That's because shearers there can sue for back injuries.'

'And the tattoos?' I ask, getting personal.

'That was Sydney for you. I was young, yeah, just seventeen. Cost a dollar fifty each back then.'

His boss, Ronny, has also been shearing for thirty years, from the age of sixteen. He followed his father into shearing. The season for blades is not as long as it once was. Gangs used to be busy from June to December; now they work from June to October, and the number of sheep has fallen from 120,000 to 80,000. Still, properties like Temple Peak and Rees Valley Stations stick to blade shearing and not just because they like the practice; the blades leave a protective layer of wool on the sheep that serves them well in a cold snap.

'Blades are holding their own,' says Ronny.

After Temple Peak, the gang has an appointment at the Rees Valley Station woolshed farther up the valley. A few more days' work there.

Lunch break is a time for checking the edge and action on the shears. Each shearer sharpens his own gear on a portable bench grinder and adds finishing touches with an oilstone. On average, the blades will need to be honed every couple of hours and quickly touched up for every sheep if need be. The grip and action are also important. Repetitive strain injury seems on the cards but no one is complaining today as far as I can tell.

As a piece of technology, blade shears rank among the oldest of metal tools. They have opposing blades like scissors but instead of being hinged at the centre, their hinge is at the back of the handle. The design is as old as the hills. Well, almost. It is said to date from the Iron Age, when iron smelting and forging was developed, over 2,000 years ago. Remarkably, the technology survives, although blade shears are really only used in a serious commercial way today in New Zealand and South Africa. There's not much blade shearing going on in England or Australia on the scale you see in the South Island high country. But Sheffield, England, a steel capital, is still manufacturing blade shears and that is where the New Zealand gangs source replacements.

With an eye on the afternoon's shearing, Mark eats his lunch in a hurry. He has work to do during the break. More hoggets need to be driven into the woolshed from the adjacent yards. He has a couple of dogs to help him plus an unusual contrivance — a red electric fence standard that has a white plastic supermarket bag attached to the end. More effective at moving the sheep than the dogs, it makes a crisp swishing noise as he waves it.

'Merinos have minds of their own,' he says after the sheep are in the shed. 'If they don't want to do something they won't do it. Give them a lead, though, and they're great followers. See over there, I had some decoy sheep penned at the back of the shed. Plus this plastic bag.'

We talk a bit, leaning on the woolshed gates. It's that kind of day, and the new lot of hoggets have gone into the shed faster than Mark thought. He's got ten minutes before the blades start up again.

Mark bought Temple Peak Station — 8,000 hectares, all of it pastoral lease — in May 1979. He was twenty-four years old and fairly new to the Head of the Lake. On his first night on the place, with the rain beating on the roof, he crawled into his sleeping bag and wondered what he'd done.

Shear poetry in motion: Jim Bool derobes a merino hogget at Temple Peak Station's woolshed.

A generation on, he and his wife, Amanda, are still there. They farm conservatively, don't overstock. They try to keep the tussock grasslands healthy. Their property is sandwiched between the larger stations of Rees Valley and Wyuna, Glenorchy's backdrop. It spans the Richardson Mountains, with the eponymous peak, 2,000 metres high, roughly in the centre of the property. The farm's back country extends about sixteen kilometres, from the homestead paddocks in the Rees Valley to a slice of the Shotover catchment.

Mark says he hasn't bought any standard superphosphate fertiliser for ten years. He applies only fine lime and modest amounts of a product called reactive rock phosphate, and the farm is producing as much wool and meat as in the past. But the tenure review process is a different matter. It is highly unsettling, and could easily upset the sustainable relationship the Hasselmans have with their pastoral leasehold land. Mark rather wishes tenure review would go away. Although it's a voluntary process, there is snarling uncertainty for high-country runholders who do not engage with it.

'Writing's on the wall,' says Mark. 'If you don't do a deal under tenure review, the rents will get you.'

And why wouldn't they want to do a deal? They like Temple Peak Station the way it is. They like protecting its natural values to the extent they can as farmers, through covenants if necessary for the pieces that are especially valuable. They don't want to see a cluster of flash houses on some newly designated 'rural lifestyle' land next door. Dilemma.

We turn to surer subjects now, Mark and I. Shearing, for one. The blades appeal to Mark's low-tech approach to life. Output per shearer is less than for a gang of machine shearers but costs work out to be more or less the same, and he thinks the sheep are better off having the extra wool on their backs. For all he knows, they might even emerge less stressed after blade shearing than if they were shorn by machines. Forty per cent of the Temple Peak clip is sold direct to the Icebreaker clothing people, who produce designer garments for outdoor pursuits.

What I especially like about Mark is his tolerance of natural hazards. That includes falcons window-shopping around his free-range chickens. He accepts them as part of the natural balance. In other areas, farmers are known to shoot falcons for preying on their hens. On a visit to England he was introduced to the ancient sport of falconry and wondered about the possibilities of using the New Zealand falcon back home. But he is having second thoughts. 'Could be worse than a team of dogs to work,' he says.

Although the remote and mountainous location of Temple Peak could have something to do with it, Mark belies the image of a modern farmer surrounded by every mod-con communication tool going. He doesn't carry a cellphone and doesn't own a television — '… never seen anything on TV I wanted to look at'. Computers are a novelty to him. He was introduced to them in 2006. His favourite website is the Victoria University of Wellington weather site, <metvuw.com>, which provides seven-day thumbnail forecasts based on satellite imagery — a handy thing if you happen to be planning three days of shearing in a climate where it can bucket down. A land-line telephone, however, Mark could not do without.

Not shy of community affairs, he chaired the Glenorchy Community Association through the years it was developing a plan for the Head of the Lake community. The plan's overarching conclusion was clear enough: retain the end-destination status of Glenorchy and the Head of the Lake. Both Mark and Amanda have long been involved with local organisations, especially the school, although Mark still wonders, after thirty years in the district, whether he has become a 'local' yet.

Amanda has been at the school on the morning I visit the woolshed, working on property issues for the board of trustees. Glenorchy School has a smaller roll than in the past. Rural schools with reducing rolls worry about their future, but in Glenorchy's case the glitzy subdivision development in the vicinity of the township is lighting its horizons. All four Hasselman children attended school in Glenorchy before leaving the district for secondary and higher education.

Around by the woolshed entrance, Amanda, back from her meeting at the school, is having a bite of lunch in the sun. Besides being a farmer alongside Mark and a director of their business, she is an artist and doing creative things with merino wool felting. Through the afternoon she will manage the stockhandling at the woolshed and yards.

I am due soon at the Rees Valley Station woolshed, up the road a few kilo-metres, to talk to Iris Scott. Mark Hasselman's first experience of the Head of the Lake was as a young musterer in the Rees Valley mountains in the late 1970s. Originally from rural South Canterbury, he was hired by Iris's late husband, Graeme Scott, and Graeme's father, Doug. I know the Scotts have been here a long time, and that Rees Valley sets a record in Head of the Lake farming circles — the station that has been in the hands of one family the longest.

Iris Scott in Rees Valley Station's woolshed … this woman deserves a DB.

er friendly face framed in long white hair, Iris Scott greets me as I drive up to the woolshed. It's a bright afternoon, made all the more colourful by the sheep in a nearby paddock. They are various shades of brown.

'They don't look like your average merino,' I say, trying to sound knowledgeable.

'You're right,' says Iris, with a half-smile that looks habitual. 'They're a small flock of crossbred coloured sheep which are kept round the woolshed for shearing demonstrations.'

'Demonstrations?'

'For visitors. It's a tourism development. We don't run it. We host it.'

When I suggest that tourists might prefer to watch shearing of merinos because they're characteristic of high-country sheep runs, Iris is quick with a response: 'Merinos are easily scratched — the wrinkly skin, you see. Blood dribbles from the scratches. Liable to upset visitors. No, the crossbreds are a better option. Want to look inside?'

Like Temple Peak's, the woolshed is a relatively well-lit modern shed, with walls clad in corrugated iron and plenty of room for an eight-strong gang of blade shearers, the rouseabouts and disco music crowding the rafters and everyone's ears. There is also space for a large standing display of the history of Rees Valley Station, its production, tourism, nature conservation and recreation values.

Of course, Rees Valley Station does have merinos — 3,000 of them. There used to be 7,000 sheep spread across the station's 18,600 hectares of pastoral-lease backcountry valleys, spurs and range tops. During an autumn muster the faces streamed with sheep, which eventually turned the yards and river flats around the Arthur's Creek woolshed up the Rees Valley into a swirling, ruffled lake of wool. Sheep numbers are lower now but the Scotts plan to get the flock back to something like 7,000 again.

Iris arrived in the district before 'Huss'. A veterinary science student from Massey University, although originally from the Waikato, she took a summer holiday job as a 'land girl' on Rees Valley Station in the late 1960s. The Scotts, father and son, knew they were getting help from a vet student over the summer but didn't reckon on a female one. Clearly, Iris made an impression despite her slight build and self-effacing manner. After returning to her Massey studies and graduating in vet science she 'came south' in February 1971 to marry Graeme and begin a life on a high-country station, one of the Otago region's most famous.

Welshman William Gilbert Rees, founder of Queenstown, established sheep farming at the Head of the Lake with a couple of partners and the blessing of the Waste Land Board, an ironically named agency in light of current land values. Rees engaged shepherds to drive flocks to the district by way of rough and sometimes troublesome trails through bracken fern and scrub, some of which had to be burnt to clear the way for the sheep. The shepherds relied on provisions from Queenstown and at one stage, when their supply of flour turned musty, they were beside themselves with hunger. Rees arrived from Queenstown by boat just in time, with a stock of pies baked by his wife.

In 1905, some forty years later, with the main means of communication still by boat, Henry Scott rode up a bridle track from Queenstown to take possession of Rees Valley Station. The Scott name appears in a list of local names on the war memorial in Mull Street that commemorates sacrifice in the Great War. Through the 1930s Great Depression and rabbit plague years, son

Kea on sheep

The first filmed evidence of kea attacking sheep came from Rees Valley Station in the mid-1990s. In an hour-long documentary about the life of kea in the high country, the TNVZ Natural History Unit included night-time shots of the alpine parrots riding on the backs of ewes and digging into the flesh with their bills. It was said they were targeting the fat layer around the kidneys. Winter, when normal kea food items are under snow, is a risky time of year but attacks can also occur in summer. Although attacked sheep do not usually die immediately, the blood poisoning or fly strike that follows days later may be fatal. Iris Scott says kea still attack her sheep, even if they have been brought to lower altitude country in autumn. Rees Valley can lose at least ten sheep a year to kea attacks. In a very bad year, the toll may be more than 150. Rees Valley sheep are vaccinated against blood poisoning and tetanus. It is administered at the time the sheep receive lice and worm drenches.

Doug Scott and his wife Jean, fought hard to stay on the property.

'Ten years without wages,' is how daughter-in-law Iris describes their experience. 'They worked for their keep, that's all.' She says that period of hardship is revisiting the high country now, with meat and wool prices depressed and steep rent increases in the wind for lessees of pastoral land. The only way to survive on the property, says Iris, is to diversify, develop alternative ways of generating income and work for wages off it. Iris has the support of her three children. In 1992, when the oldest was only sixteen, Iris's husband, Graeme died. She then had three school-age children to bring up and a huge farm to run.

After the tour of the woolshed, Iris and I make our way to the homestead down on the flats, which, like the house on Mount Earnslaw Station, has no pretension to material wealth but is continuously lived in. Over a cuppa I discuss the challenges facing the Scott family.

Iris speaks in a quiet, measured way borne of self-belief sharpened at many a high-country forum. There is a sparkle in her eye, too, not diminished by the pressures of managing a large property. Few women run sheep farms this big. Iris Scott is a well-known name among the 'Feds' — Federated Farmers Inc. — and the Landcare Group movement. She not only asserts the right of high-country farming to exist but is also clear about its benefits to nation and society. The information panels back at the woolshed — a busy mosaic of photographs and text, assembled by Amanda Hasselman — express a determination to get the message across. Pastoral runs are not just about the meat and wool export trade; they embody significant landscapes, water quality, recreational opportunity, tourism activity. And they are the backdrop for cultural symbols such as Speight's beer, sheep dogs and drover raincoats.

But times are tough.

'Right now this property won't support one income let alone four. We've all got other jobs, and it's going to be like that for a while.'

Kate, the eldest daughter, named for her industrious great-grandmother, Henry's wife, works part-time in the Glenorchy School office and public library and helps Iris with much of the farm work; Diane has had café and bus-driving jobs; and the youngest member of the family, Eric, is based in Queenstown and has his sights set on flying helicopters. All three are keen to see Rees Valley Station remain in Scott family ownership. Even their mother has to supplement farm income with jobs off-property. She washes dishes part-time at the exclusive luxury lodge just south of Glenorchy, Blanket Bay, and does occasional veterinary jobs around the district, although more often as a favour than for income.

The Scotts initiated tourism on the station a while back. Ventures have to be small-scale, on the family's terms and compatible with pastoral lease farming. Besides shearing demonstrations, there is a horse-trekking business operating from the homestead area. A skifield is available in winter (helicopter access, rope tow and a hut at 1,650 metres, accommodating ten people at a time) high up in the Richardson Mountains near the Invincible Creek headwaters. There are eco-tours, also with helicopter access, for botanists and entomologists keen to explore the alpine zone, and four-wheel-drive Landrover trips along the valley floor, offered to visitors by Glenorchy identity Dick Watson.

A few years back the Scotts entered into a tenure review process with the government agency, Land Information New Zealand (LINZ). With only 250 hectares of freehold in the homestead area, the station is almost entirely pastoral lease. It takes in the northern end of the Richardson Mountains, its parallel valleys and intervening spurs, almost all the way to the Rees Saddle. The largest paddocks run for kilometres from the valley floor to the range tops.

Iris was keen to see whether the tenure review process was flexible and innovative, whether it would accept a new way of looking at managing the high country. Financial security was not a motive. In the mid-1990s she turned down an offer of $12 million for Rees Valley Station. It wasn't for sale.

Iris, backed up by her children, proposed to LINZ that the entire station be placed under a covenant that would limit grazing, burn-offs and fertiliser applications and protect natural values. 'We put the stewardship case, where profit is secondary to caring for the land,' says Iris. 'Maintaining water quality, biodiversity, that sort of thing. At the same time, allowing for appropriate forms of recreation and tourism — pretty much what we do now. Grazing at high altitude would be at very low stocking rates, and we'd put no pressure on the dark faces and the patches of forest. There'd be no subdivision for lifestyle houses. As far as the DOC interest goes, there's nothing on Rees Valley that is not already well represented in the national park and adjacent conservation land. Rees Valley is like a buffer zone for Mount Aspiring National Park, a line of defence against invasion by weeds and pests.'

The government negotiators saw things differently. They wanted most of the pastoral lease to be managed by the Department of Conservation. A letter arrived from LINZ in December 2007, a couple of days before my visit. It stated: '… the parties are at an impasse'. There would be no deal. LINZ had decided to discontinue the tenure review of Rees Valley Station.

Iris is philosophical. It is what she expects from an official process unable to deal creatively in what is best for the high country. I tell her the Lark would sympathise with her thoughts about treading lightly on the high country … about not putting lines on maps and separating areas of production from areas of conservation (except in the case of rare habitats or plant life requiring full protection) … about integrating human pursuits sustainably with nature … about renewal. Iris will try other avenues. Giving up is not in her nature. She will continue politicking and continue to air her views publicly. Her recent reappointment to the Otago Conservation Board by the Minister of Conservation says a lot about her interest in bridging the production/conservation arguments.

The no-deal letter from LINZ and the threat of rent increases confirm for her a pattern of government antipathy towards high-country farming that she says goes back to the late 1980s, when a government agency accused high-country farmers of polluting waterways. 'You have to remember this was a time when cities all over New Zealand were pumping raw sewage directly into estuaries and the ocean.'

Scottish pioneers in Otago, including my own, knew all about the Highland Clearances back home. 'High-Country Clearances' is what the tenure review process is being labelled in the twenty-first century by some leaders of the farming community.

Dick Watson, owner-operator of a four-wheel drive tour business, Mountainland Rovers, can talk with some authority about the nature of the rocks and minerals at the Head of the Lake. He has moved plenty of them. As a bulldozer driver, he put in the Kinloch-Greenstone Road in the early 1980s and realigned sections of the Queenstown-Glenorchy Road. He also pushed rocks and rubble around at the scheelite mines above Glenorchy, and rattled countless tonnes of river gravels through a floating dredge in the Buckler Burn and Precipice Creek while gold mining in the late 'eighties: best strike, half an ounce of gold in one hour.

Dick's family connections go back a long way here. He is a fifth-generation descendant of the first proprietor of the Glenorchy Hotel, Thomas Wilson. Thomas ran tours into the Rees Valley from Glenorchy. Ditto Dick. But instead of horse and buggy, his mode of transport is a Landrover. It's no ordinary four-wheel drive, certainly not in the same mould as the shiny SUVs that inhabit supermarket carparks and hardly get off tarseal. Dick's vehicle is a long-wheelbase 1997 Landrover Defender, a chunky, no-frills model.

I was in the Rees Valley some years back, tramping the Rees-Dart, and look forward to an opportunity to experience it through Dick's eyes. I'm pleased no one else is booked on my tour. I plan on asking questions no Asian backpacker would dream of asking. Dick picks me up at 9 a.m. from my motel with a solid handshake and a characteristic southern New Zealand rolling of the Rs, even in words that don't contain the letter.

'Good to meet yer,' he says in a gravely voice. He has tousled hair, white enough to suggest middle age, and a square-jawed, no-nonsense look about him — like his vehicle.

'Likewise,' I return. 'Rain on the way?'

Stoat-buster: Dick Watson faces up to Enemy No. 1 for local birds.

'We'll be jake for a couple of hours.' Dick starts up the ten-year-old diesel motor. I continue conversation on the weather theme: 'Creeks and river okay?'

'Yeah, no problem. The new snow's stored most of the rain.'

I lever myself into the passenger seat in the front and we drive off towards the intersection by the town's Recreation Ground, which hosts rugby, golf and horse racing, but only one code at a time. Dick drives straight over the top of the roundabout with a terse comment echoing the local barman's: 'That's been put in for visitors.'

Instead of following the road towards the Rees Valley he swings through the monumental gates of the Glenorchy Recreation Ground and leans forward over the wheel, his right arm cuddling it.

'Need to check something.' He looks towards the near corner of the ground.

I know it'll be pounded by horses' hooves on the first Saturday in January — the Glenorchy Races. 'We put down new grass seed here for the next races. Then hundreds of chaffinches arrived and ate the seed, so we had to re-sow it. Just checking the strike. Looks promising.'

Dick was one of the instigators of the community-run Glenorchy races back in the early 1960s and he hasn't missed a race day since. He does his bit for the local community, most recently signing up as a volunteer fireman — 'A younger man's game, but the brigade was short.'

Dick is the epitome of a Head of the Lake all-rounder. He has been a musterer, bulldozer driver, gold dredge operator, jetboat driver, shearer, eeler, venison hunter, possum hunter, hotel proprietor (four years running his great-great-grandfather's hotel) and, most recently, through the Mountainland Rovers business he set up in 2003, a four-wheel drive tour guide and stoat-trapping nature conservationist, about which I figure I'll be learning a good deal today.

It's not long before he is hitting his stride as a tour guide with his lone passenger. Beyond Twelve Mile Creek and the powerhouse serving Glenorchy by the bridge, Rees Valley Road travels along a raised bench through regenerating shrubland. Dick stops to describe the scene: in the foreground, the Rees River split into several channels across its gravel bed, and the flat paddocks of Mount Earnslaw Station surrounding knobbly, glacier-smoothed Camp Hill; in the distance, mountains under masses of dark-grey cloud.

'After the last ice age all this flat land in front of us was a lake,' says Dick. 'These terraces, they hark back to a time when Lake Wakatipu was a lot higher and extended a fair way up the Rees and Dart Valleys.'

He talks of the Rees men who introduced sheep, the surveyors under McKerrow who added more names to the landscape, and the 'banker' floods. In a big flood the rivers form a sheet of water bank to bank. Volumes in the Dart River average less than one hundred cubic metres per second but on the day of the Glenorchy Races in January, 1994, the Dart hit an estimated 2,200 cumecs.

Camp Hill was the site of a moa-hunter encampment a long time ago. There is talk of human occupation taking a new turn through a subdivision development for about thirty houses. Dick is upset.

'I'm not a big fan of subdivisions and definitely against this one. Imagine stopping here in the future and having a bunch of houses in the middle of this glorious view of the mountains.'

Neither is he a fan of the Milford-Dart tunnel project. He calls it 'a crazy thing', and an example of Queenstown 'putting its big foot on us'.

Invincible Creek is the next stop. Here, tour guide becomes stoat-trapper. Dick dives into the fern beside the bridge to check one of the one hundred-odd traps deployed at intervals a long way into the Rees Valley. A wooden box the size of a large shoe box, but longer, is baited with hen's eggs. Neck-breaking steel kill-traps are set on either side of the eggs. The project, titled 'Bring Back Our Birds', began in 2004 after Dick realised that stoats were decimating birdlife in the area, especially the banded dotterels, black-fronted terns, wrybills and South Island pied oystercatchers that nest on the open gravel islands in the river-bed. Besides the traps up the Rees Valley his project is setting them in downstream areas, too. He's got a new trap going into a creek at Paradise tomorrow.

'I got thinking about what my grandkids would lose,' he says. 'I was amazed at the response when I advertised for sponsors. Dozens of people offered to pay for a trap and a supermarket said it would donate the eggs.'

In the first year Dick and his volunteer stoat-busters would find stoats in just about every trap inspected. The traps are all mapped on a GPS system for easy monitoring. Dick checks a number of them on his regular tours up the Rees Valley but is careful not to offend clients if a trap has done its job. Asian women in particular are sensitive to the killing.

A handful of gold

The Invincible Gold Mine operated for about ten years at the end of the nineteenth century. Legend has it that gold was discovered in the vicinity by a shepherd called McDougall, who worked for runholder Rees. He was tending sheep on a steep bank of the Invincible Creek when he stumbled, grabbed a tussock to break his fall and pulled the plant out by its roots. The exposed gritty soil was aglitter with gold fines.

Above Invincible Creek, Rees Valley Road passes through a forested gorge, beyond which the valley opens up again — river flats to gladden the eye of Rees's men. Another valley 'door' swings shut. Near here Dick has stopped again to point out a woodland of mature matagouri bushes laden with old man's beard moss. The matagouri have twisted, craggy trunks and branches that are conspicuous because of the light foliage, and according to Dick these very bushes were the inspiration to the designers of the race of giant walking/talking trees in *The Lord of the Rings* series of movies, including Treebeard of the Forest of Fangorn.

Muddy Creek is where tarseal motorists and faint-hearted four-wheel drives turn back. Creek and river crossings come thick and fast beyond this point. At the first ford of the river, which involves mounting a gravel bank on the far side, I lift my camera bag off the floor in case the water comes inside the cab.

'She's designed to let in water,' says my guide. 'That way we won't float downstream.'

He knows what he's talking about. Dick's enthusiasm for Landrovers prompted him to organise a Landrover rally in 2002. It attracted 300 vehicles from around New Zealand. A highlight was a trip up the Rees Valley, with the permission of the Scotts, and from that trip Dick got the idea for four-wheel drive nature tours describing the landforms, forest, birdlife and the ecology of braided rivers. He had no hesitation choosing the 1997 Defender for the job.

'Great in rivers,' he says. 'Gearbox is watertight — you can't beat it for river crossings.'

I note the fuel gauge is touching the red zone. I point this out.

'Uses hardly any diesel on a trip,' says Dick. 'We're really only idling along. No carbon footprint to speak of.'

Stoat footprints, though, are fatal signs for the braided-river birds breeding here. Apart from moving swiftly over land, stoats swim. They can easily access the gravel islands of the Rees River. Following wheel tracks across one of the islands on our way upstream, we pause to look out for a banded dotterel nest Dick has seen on a previous trip. On cue, the little bird, the colour of the stones and with black and brown breeding bands across its chest, scurries across the tracks ahead of us, dangling a wing in a decoy strategy aimed to entice us away from its nest.

The door of the valley
Swings shut behind.
But in the next gully
Who knows but I'll find
The colour to make all tongues wag.

From 'The Bush',
Arawata Bill: A Sequence of Poems,
by Denis Glover, 1953

Humboldt Mountains and the Glenorchy Lagoons.

'You watch, she'll take a look at us then think, "Oh, it's okay, it's only old Dick", and go back to the nest.'

Which the dotterel duly does. The bird returns to hunker down on the gravels beside a cushion plant, no longer recognisable as a bird. Dick reckons the birdlife is benefitting from the trapping. For evidence, he tells me about a pair of paradise shelducks that raised eighteen young last season. The skylarks are more plentiful than ever, too, and even on a dull day like this one, when you'd wonder what there was to chirrup about, the larks are in the air and broadcasting their lyrical song, the longest bird song of all.

At Arthurs Creek, we stop at my request to take a look at the woolshed. Not large and no longer in use, it is clad in unpainted corrugated iron. There is space on the boards for two shearers but the Lister diesel motor looks a bit seized up. The Arthurs Creek musterers' huts are located near a patch of mountain beech, reminding me of a story I heard from Glenorchy resident Pat Gollop, who worked on Rees Valley Station as a musterer between spells of scheelite mining with his father in the 1950s and 1960s. A mustering gang could spend a week here. They would put thousands of sheep through a dip. They'd eat sheep meat morning, noon and night — greasy chops for breakfast, cold meat for lunch, roast mutton for the evening meal. There were rabbits by the thousand in the valley. In the winter of 1946, a couple of rabbiters based at Arthurs Creek killed 11,000 of them, according to Dick.

Twenty kilometres from Glenorchy, the Arthurs Creek woolshed is maintained as an emergency shelter on Rees Valley Station. There is an emergency radio inside it, with spare batteries. Sometimes trampers doing the Rees-Dart circuit or mountaineers tackling the tops get into trouble. I imagine the Lark might spend a night here on his travels. He's spoken of this spot and another backcountry musterers' base as well — Big Devil Hut, up Twenty-five Mile Creek, although Iris Scott tells me it is locked these days. Inside the Arthurs Creek woolshed a pile of hay suggests someone dossed down recently. Possums, too, have spent time here, judging by the dung scattered about the dark interior.

Below the woolshed, Dick checks a trap. There is a stoat in it, freshly killed. The bared teeth suggest a last defiant act. The thick brown fur is no match for the jaws of the trap. He removes it, and points out the long tail's furry black tip. Dick has a theory about the black tip I haven't heard before. 'It's for distracting predators like hawks or falcons,' he says. 'They're more likely to go for a waving black object than the head end.' I am not so sure about that. I doubt if falcons of whatever species, European peregrine or the endemic New Zealand falcon, would be fooled. We drive farther up the valley and Dick points out that falcons are nesting in the beech trees close to the river.

Opposite Lennox Falls, the turn-round point on the trip, I talk about Dave Sharpe's 1985 sighting of a South Island kōkako at the forest edge. I ask Dick if he has any kōkako stories. Would he recognise one? He says he probably wouldn't. But he does have a kākāpō tale.

In the winter of 1961, Dick was deer shooting in the Dart Valley. Between Daley's Flat and Cattle Flat, he came upon two plump green birds moving slowly over mossy ground at the edge of the forest. He had never seen birds of their ilk before. Fascinated, he watched them climb on a log, still grubbing at moss. They crawled around the log, clinging like parrots. The description certainly fits kākāpō, and later, when he related the story to Lloyd Veint at Arcadia Station, Lloyd told him he'd seen similar birds in the Dart forest. Kākāpō were last reported in the wild in Fiordland in the 1980s. They are now presumed to be extinct on mainland New Zealand. But unlike South Island kōkako, a highly-managed breeding population of kākāpō survives on Codfish Island near Stewart Island.

We turn back for Glenorchy, and with less commentary coming from Dick I quiz him further about his history at the Head of the Lake. A teenager in the 1950s, living at Nightcaps, and then in Dunedin, he used to visit his uncle, Wattie Watson, at Routeburn Station, on the Kinloch side of the lake — boat access only. Like others of his generation, Dick has vivid memories of the lake steamer, *Ben Lomond*: 'She was terrible in a storm'. The vessel rolled violently. He remembers the lifeboats swinging alarmingly on their davits. In the early 1960s, he returned to Routeburn Station to work as a farm hand.

In Dick Watson's youth, the Kinloch side of the lake was an even remoter experience than Glenorchy. And if you lived on the farms to the south of Kinloch, you had no formed roads, no phone and no power, and as far as the young Elfin Shaw, of Elfin Bay Station, was concerned, no worries either.

South Island robin, Dart Valley. GILBERT VAN REENEN/CLEAN GREEN IMAGES

CHAPTER 7

The Far Side

A generation before Iris Scott came to Rees Valley Station to work as a land girl, Elfin Shaw and her older sister Betty were doing equivalent work on one of New Zealand's most isolated farms — Elfin Bay Station, Lake Wakatipu. Elfin's given names were June Laura. She acquired the nickname after the family moved to the lake station from a dairy farm at Mosgiel in 1929, when she was just a year old.

Elfin Bay is on the far side of the lake, about opposite Pig Island/Matau. The mouth of the Greenstone River is a couple of kilometres to the north. Although farm tracks connected Elfin Bay to Kinloch in the north and Mount Nicholas Station in the south, the Shaws relied mainly on the steamer service from Queenstown — three times a week in summer, two times in winter — to keep them in touch with the outside world. Elfin and her sister had a governess and in the 1930s took their 3 Rs education by correspondence until their parents decided they should go to school in Queenstown.

The farm, which ran 3,000 merinos, was itself a learning experience for the girls. They rode horses and young heifers. They helped their father, George, with stock work, the vegetable garden and orchard, and their mother, Annie, with preserving the fruit and vegies. The two girls went deer hunting with .303 rifles from an age their father thought safe, and they had adventures — like the time they were returning in the station's dinghy with their dad, after a visit to Mount Creighton Station on the other side of the lake, and got lost in fog. They were becalmed for an hour or two till it lifted.

The local birdlife became entertainment. They had a paradise shelduck as a pet. Elfin was fascinated by how a paradise duck parent could transport ducklings on its back. She even saw an adult bird ferry young from its forest-edge nest site to the lake shore by flying them three or four at a time. A kea became a pet, too. To stop it getting into mischief, the family kept it on a chain. One day they let the kea go. It was chased out of sight by a harrier hawk or falcon. Elfin thought that was the end of it. About three weeks later, their father was riding back from Mount Nicholas Station when he saw a solitary and sad-looking kea beside the lakeshore track at Black Gorge Creek, five kilometres south of Elfin Bay. It was the family pet, and starving. George picked it up and brought it home to the delight of his younger daughter.

When Elfin came back from secondary school in Dunedin, where she boarded, the world was at war and most of the district's able-bodied men had gone to the battlefields of North Africa and Europe. The Shaw sisters would get pocket money from selling red-deer skins. Deer tails also found a market — a Chinese man in Dunedin, who wanted them for medicinal use. Rabbits were another source of income. The skins were shipped out to a processing plant in Cromwell. With no power available for machine shearing, the sisters took on blade shearing with their father. Elfin's best daily tally shearing ewes was seventy-eight. She became a full-blown farm hand on Elfin Bay Station following the example of her older sister, Betty, who officially joined the army of land girls. Elfin worked for no pay for about seven years until she left the farm to get married. Her jobs included driving cattle from the Greenstone Valley to the saleyards at Lorneville in Southland. It took a week to get them delivered and three days to ride home.

Elfin never knew how it was to live on a farm with electric power till 1950, when she married a Southland farmer, Gordon McDonald, and moved to Dipton. She was twenty-two.

Of the many childhood memories of station life that Elfin Shaw took with her into the outside world, the Arawata Bill years have a special kind of glow. Bill O'Leary stayed at Elfin Bay Station for a few weeks or months at a time from about 1932. He spent several winters there between bouts of prospecting and bushranging in the mountains and valleys out west during the warmer months. Despite his advancing years and snow-white beard,

Girl power: sisters Elfin (centre) and Betty Shaw help their father, George (Gi), with blade shearing at Elfin Bay Station during World War II. SHAW FAMILY COLLECTION

he was still active in the hills and would tell his hosts on the western side of the lake — the Cooks and Groves at Routeburn, the Bryants at Kinloch and the Shaws at Elfin Bay — stories of mineral riches to be found in the Red Hills and other wilderness areas of South Westland. The treasure he spoke of, besides gold, included rubies, garnets, copper, asbestos and oil.

At first, to the young Shaw girls, he was a scary old man who would appear suddenly out of nowhere. But as the years passed and they became used to his quiet and kindly presence, he was as welcome as Santa Claus, and a little like him, too, when he produced wrinkled brown bags of blackballs and peppermints. It didn't matter that the sweets had travelled around with him a long time and were showing signs of ageing. He'd arrive on his horse Dolly, a bay mare with a prominent white blaze. She would be loaded with sacks and saddlebags. The girls noticed he always wore a fob watch, which was attached to a shiny gold chain and tucked into the waistcoat of his dark suit. His rounded nose and chubby cheeks made him look parrot- or owl-faced.

At Elfin Bay Station, Bill was given the use of an annexe near the four-bedroom homestead. It had a kitchen and bathroom, bedroom and bunkroom. It was also used by visitors who came by steamer or by horse from adjacent sheep and cattle stations. Bill stayed weeks or a couple of months at a time, and worked for his food and lodging, tending the garden and orchard, and cutting and stacking firewood.

To find out first-hand about those times, I get in touch with Elfin McDonald (née Shaw). Approaching eighty now, she lives in a brick bungalow in a relatively new northern suburb of Timaru, with a school on one side and a grass paddock on another, a rural outlook pleasing to her eye. A daughter lives nearby.

Still sprightly and exuberant, Elfin welcomes me into her living room. Books about the Head of the Lake are piled high on the dining table. She apologises for not having her photos of her Elfin Bay days available — they're in storage — and another thing, she has a housekeeper and district nurse due this morning but they won't be a bother.

Elfin says she was Arawata Bill's favourite. She and her sister, Betty, never called him by that name. To them, he was always 'Mr O'Leary' or just 'Mr'. He would take the girls for rides on Dolly, and let them catch and feed her. In the evenings, he would join the family for dinner and tell them stories of his travels and his treasure-seeking. Although the Shaws never saw much in the way of precious stones, Elfin recalls a demonstration involving shale oil, which he collected in bottles:

'One time Bill brought back some oil from the Red Hills or somewhere, and put a little bit in a saucer and lit it. That amazed us girls. Really, he was a cheerful old man underneath the shyness. Sometimes, if there was some music going, he would break out into a dance, even inside the house — he did a sort of Highland Fling. Loved the old songs.'

The girls used to notice him scratching occasionally at his clothing and hear him complaining to their parents of the damnable 'birch itch'. He chose a patch of manuka as a camp site in the lower Greenstone Valley near Lake Rere as a relief from beech trees, which he said caused the skin problem. Elfin is not so sure the beech was to blame, and wonders if he suffered dermatitis caused by a diet deficiency, perhaps a lack of fresh fruit and vegetables on his long expeditions, or something else altogether.

Cleanliness was not an issue. Bill O'Leary was fussy about having a wash and making himself respectable for dinner, and he was always washing his clothes and hanging them out to dry.

Tribal property

E lfin Bay, Greenstone and Routeburn Stations were purchased by the government and given to the South Island's Tahu people, through Te Runanganui o Ngai Tahu, in part settlement of the claims under the Treaty of Waitangi settlement. That settlement, enshrined in legislation, was agreed to by the Crown and Ngai Tahu in 1998. The stations are still working farms, although the mountain tops, Ka Whenua Roimata (Land of Tears), have since been gifted back to the people of New Zealand by Ngai Tahu.

I ask Elfin if she remembers anything about Bill and Dolly sometimes arriving at Elfin Bay Station with 'portable oven saddle bags' containing cooked pigeons. There is an intriguing reference to this in Ian Dougherty's excellent biography of the legendary prospector, *Arawata Bill*, and the story is picked up in a tribute to the lone prospector at the information kiosk at Chinaman's Bluff on the Rees-Dart track. There, the panel describing Arawata Bill talks of his using a 'portable hangi' to carry food between camps. Can Elfin shed any light on this? It seems far-fetched. How would Dolly cope with the weight of the stones let alone their heat?

'It happened like this,' says Elfin. 'Somewhere on the way back from the Hollyford, Bill and perhaps one of the McKenzie fellows from Martins Bay would catch a few native pigeons. The Rats Nest Hut might be one place, halfway up the Greenstone Valley to Howden. In the morning they'd stuff the pigeons with a bit of salt and some fat or butter. They'd take a few hot stones they'd left overnight in the fireplace in the hut, not large stones, and poke them inside the birds so the stones were sort of insulated. Then they'd wrap up the birds and the stones in a sugar bag or two and put them in the saddle bags, and by the time they got to our place, the pigeons had been slow-cooked through. Delicious, they were, too.'

Elfin's mother would have the treat on the table that evening, with home-grown potatoes and peas. And Dolly didn't suffer at all, it seems, from the weight and heat of normal hangi stones.

olly lived a long time. Bill O'Leary had her for about half of the forty-odd years he was roaming the wild west. He bought her for £5 in South Westland, at Waipara in the Arawhata catchment, when she was three years old. Bill was devoted to her, and the feeling, from all accounts, was mutual. Elfin reckons the packhorse was 'a quarter draught', which explains Dolly's tolerance of heavy loads and long days hauling over alpine passes. At Elfin Bay Station she was allowed to graze with the station horses but generally she kept to herself. In that respect she was a match for her master.

The manner of her death has become the stuff of legend. There are stories of her stumbling in mountain terrain and breaking a leg. An illustration published in 1948 in the London-based *Wide World Magazine* portrays O'Leary, who died the previous year in Dunedin, clearly anguished about having to shoot the fallen horse. The painting accompanied an article by Dunedin correspondent Harry Fortune, a newspaper subeditor, who had written an article for the same magazine in 1935 from second-hand reports about the daring exploits of the lone 'Down Under' prospector.

Some reports portrayed Dolly's own courage. On one trip into the mountains in the 1930s, Bill fell over a twenty-metre cliff and after he had dragged himself back up, Dolly was there to carry her badly hurt master over fifty kilometres back to the Head of the Lake, for transfer to hospital. They were bred tough, the pair of them.

Mercy-shot after breaking a leg is the consistent version of how she died. But there is confusion about where she died and when. Can Elfin shed any light?

'All I heard was that Dolly put a leg through bridge timbers somewhere around the Head of the Lake, and she had to be put down because she was stuck with a broken leg.'

From all accounts, Bill O'Leary undertook his last long expedition with Dolly to the Hollyford about 1938. Around this time Christchurch photographer Thelma Kent portrayed the stout-legged horse, alive and loaded up, in three photographs. They are the classic images of a legend. Her master is standing beside her, in suit and gumboots, with his hat on his head in two shots and resting on Dolly's load in the third. The load is so high he has to reach up to place his hat on it. There is a length of flax in his hand, an extension of the rope reins, presumably to make it easier to lead the horse on foot.

Arawata Bill told Elfin Shaw, his 'favourite', that she could have Dolly, her saddle and bridle but the horse was dead before he left the Head of the Lake. Someone reportedly stole her saddle. With Elfin away at boarding school in Dunedin the bridle remained at Elfin Bay Station. Over the years it grew stiff without oiling and Dolly's use of it.

Says Elfin: 'The leather got brittle and split. It wasn't much use in the end.'

The memory is strong, though. In a district renowned for its horses and horse-racing to this day, Dolly is an equine hero figure, just as her master is a legend among the early prospectors of South Westland and the mountains and valleys at the Head of the Lake.

Dolly was the robust kind of high-country horse I imagine might have been an odds-on contender at the Glenorchy Races, had she been born in the latter half of the twentieth century. I'll be able to check this out soon enough. Glenorchy's famous horse races are coming up. The event is held every year on the first Saturday in January. I'm wondering if the Lark will turn up for it.

In the meantime, though, I have an appointment in the lower Routeburn. It's at the footbridge to Lake Sylvan, next to the old Cook sawmill site and the paddocks where Dolly once grazed with the twenty to thirty mill horses.

Barry Lawrence is among a breed I'd call committed friends of nature. You can tell them apart by the hours they volunteer for threatened species work and habitat protection. A former high school teacher, he works for the Department of Conservation at Queenstown, and dishes out business cards that state he is managing biodiversity assets (as if continuously desk-bound, listing assets on a balance sheet with or without qualified audits!). Barry is as down to earth, and about as close to it, as any of the Wakatipu farmers. From previous contacts with him, before he joined DOC on a permanent basis, I know he has freely given large chunks of time to nature conservation in the past, mohua protection in particular. His job now includes protecting mohua, kākā, kākāriki, blue duck and robin populations on conservation land at the Head of the Lake. I am keen to meet him in the field, get a handle on the 'assets' and hear what he's doing to safeguard them. We arrange to meet at the Lake Sylvan carpark off the road to the Routeburn Shelter, a popular place for campers, trampers and sandflies.

It's a cool, clear afternoon with a dusting of snow on the tops, rather late for the time of year. In these conditions, and with no rain imminent, there is only one other vehicle — not Barry's — at the riverside carpark. Here the river's gravel delta begins to fan out, but the river is still entrenched, making it a reasonable place for siting a swing bridge. There are various signs for campers, including one at the edge of the beech forest that warns against camping under the trees. Apparently wild winds in the past have torn branches off, damaging tents. Things can go bump in the night around here.

But this is more than a gathering point for day-trippers, campers and trampers. If you could quickly survey all the human activity at the Head of the Lake going back to the first people, you'd see that it was a nerve centre. It formed part of a greenstone trail to the West Coast for the Waitaha people, who were the moa-hunters and workers of pounamu. It saw explorer Patrick Caples pass by, on foot and by himself, heading for the Harris Saddle — the first European to reach the west coast from the Wakatipu catchment. From the late 1800s, it witnessed columns of sight-seeing visitors who came on horse back or in horse-drawn buggies to experience the thundering Routeburn Gorge, the mid-altitude grassy river flats and the tarns and subalpine vegetation above the tree line. Later on, open-roofed buses brought visitors in droves. The area also hosted a sawmill and associated logging tramline in the early part of the twentieth century that converted magnificent specimens of red beech from the Lake Sylvan flatland into building timber. Then came generations of farmed sheep and cattle, and nesting falcons. Today, the human cavalcade includes trekkers wielding digital cameras and conservationists seeking to rid the forest of fur. It's a strategic area, the Sylvan carpark.

Barry pulls in, greyer than I remember and dressed equally well for a cold snap and fieldwork. He carries a radio, binoculars and clipboard. South Island robins/toutouwai are the monitoring target today. He wants to walk a 400-metre transect through the forest and record how many robins show up, and has invited me along.

The robins are not listed as endangered yet but Barry is clearly worried about

Barry Lawrence ... friend of nature.

them. Bird populations under threat can suddenly collapse in areas where predator numbers have a history of exploding — and this is one such area. Stoats, ship (black) rats and mice are an ever-present menace but, on the positive side, the threat reduces in proportion to their numbers. Such reductions happen when food gets short and trapping and poisoning operations are effective.

In 2006, the beech trees here seeded en masse as they do periodically, say, every three to five years. Mouse and rat numbers went ballistic. As we follow the Lake Sylvan track into the forest, Barry says: 'In here you'd see a mouse every few steps, and a rat about every hundred. The mice were hoovering the forest floor for insects and anything they could find to eat. If we can keep the mice and rats under control, the stoats won't get as bad. I believe ship rats are the wild card — get them and we will be on top of the rest. They're very good tree climbers.'

What we're walking through at the start of the track is a tall forest of red and

South Island robin … too confiding. GILBERT VAN REENEN/CLEAN GREEN IMAGES

mountain beech that is silent except for twittering chaffinches high up and some way off. The understorey is as spacious as a woodland or planted forest. It's coming up one hundred years since the area was logged, with a corduroy tramline slowly fading into the forest floor a reminder of its industrial past. The forest has regrown but the trees are mostly same-age and form a compact canopy. There are few light wells to encourage naturally-staggered regeneration, and the understorey is sparse, browsed out by deer and other animals. Moss and small flat ferns dominate the ground cover. Decaying stumps convey a graveyard image. I feel slightly uncomfortable here, as if the ghosts of laughing owl, kiwi, kōkako and other species lost to it are trying to make themselves heard.

Barry seems to be reading my mind. He says: 'It's not like this all the way out to the lake. You come across fairly dense patches. A new American study has confirmed that where there's good understorey you'll get good bird life.'

'Makes sense.'

'Intuitively, yes, but it's good to have the science backing it up.'

Mohua, the vulnerable yellowheads, inhabit this forest in frolicking families, although they are quiet or absent today, and kākāriki, the yellow-crowned parakeets, also find nest holes in the trees in this forest. Even kākā are sometimes found here. But robins are what we have come about. In twenty minutes we arrive at the preordained bait line. It is angling away from the walking track, a straight line marked by blue plastic triangles heading for the Dart River. We go crunching over broken branches on a mostly spongy surface. The bait stations are plastic tunnels. Before a poisoning operation, they will be loaded with bait to get the rodents accustomed to eating it. We are using these stations today merely as a basis for monitoring robins.

At each bait station, Barry pulls a plastic container from his jacket pocket and removes a few mealy worms, brown and wriggling. They have been sent from Auckland where they are produced for purposes such as this. He puts a small handful down on the top of each tunnel then claps his hands twice, muffled thuds that remind me of the way the kava ceremonies are conducted in Fiji and Tonga.

'A couple of claps should draw in any robins within earshot,' Barry says. The local robins are being taught to associate the claps with a feed of worms. By this time the calls of the ubiquitous chaffinch have been joined by the circular songs of the grey warbler and the equally engaging brown creeper, bush birds of similar size and not as much under threat of predation as the robins or mohua.

We are almost at the end of the bait line before a robin shows up. Barry has his eye in. He sees it before I do. Robins have a distinctive call but when they choose not to utter it they are simply winged silence. After a moment's sideways contemplation of the two intruders into its territory, it makes straight for the bait station, where the mealy worms are dispersing in various directions. Barry says the cold will get the worms if the robins don't. But our lone robin is in hot pursuit of them. It holds them crossways in its bill, like a puffin feeding on sardines, before flying off to a broken-off sapling with its haul.

'He'll be thinking about caching the worms,' says Barry. 'Somewhere up high.'

We leave the robin to its windfall. One robin does not a summer or a survey make. It is a lone statistic in a long-term monitoring programme that will inform Barry and his colleagues about predation rates and population dynamics, and what to expect in the mohua community, which is rather more difficult to keep tabs on.

We make our way back to the old tramline, which is separate from the walking track. The tramline leads us to the left bank of the Routeburn a couple of hundred metres downstream from the foot bridge. All that remains of the logging bridge that once spanned the river at this point are a few broken-down wooden piles. On the opposite bank, well above normal river levels, red beech logs as long as whales lie stranded there after being swept down in massive floods in the past. Under one of these logs a pair of falcons made a nest in recent times, raised a couple of young and, unsuspectingly, made a statement about the natural rhythms of the area — that given a fighting chance, native species can bounce back even if displaced for a good deal of time by logging, farming or other human endeavour.

But will a South Island kōkako ever be seen or heard around here again? Such a bird was reported from the lower Routeburn forest in the mid-nineties. The Lark says don't write them off. I agree.

Canada geese at Dart River.

Thundering down the back straight in the relay race.

CHAPTER 8

The Races

The burly ticket-seller greeting vehicles arriving at the Glenorchy Recreation Ground main gate sets the tone for the day: country-casual and hard-case.

'When's the first race due to start?' I ask.

'Any time soon — we're on Glenorchy Time.'

He dishes out a dark-red sticker that says 'Yes, I've paid — Lakeside Football Club, Races '08', and a programme, and I park with the other punters on the rugby field inside the race track, not far from a set of rusty goalposts. It's mid-morning. The mercury is climbing, and the parched grass for parking on looks alarmingly treeless and therefore shadeless.

In the cordoned-off street next to the ground the horses are tied up to fences and trees, each carrying a large identification number on its hindquarters. Their riders, many of them women, are busy checking saddles and bridles, and chatting animatedly as if getting some important new gossip about goings-on in local equine social circles — straight from the horse's mouth. They are wearing black T-shirts with pink lettering on the back. It says: 'Ride it like you stole it!'

Towards 11 o'clock, the public-address system starts up — two male voices, rather similar, who introduce themselves as 'Grant and Ferg — the Odd Couple'. They are radio announcers from Queenstown, a double act with quick-fire repartee and clearly not new to providing commentary for this event.

The 'modern' Glenorchy Races began as a fundraiser for the Lakeside Football Club, aka the Glenorchy Rugby Club, in 1962, growing out of an annual sports day to become a legend among the country's horse-racing carnivals. Glenorchy race days go back over a century, with gaps of a few years here and there. Some of the horses used to be barged to the Head of the Lake from the sheep and cattle stations surrounding it. Previewing the 2008 event, the Queenstown weekly newspaper is describing the Glenorchy Races as 'New Zealand's most rustic race meeting'. This is horse-heaven after all, a district in which horses just about outnumber people and where, in the past, they have smoothed the way for prospectors, pastoralists and tourists dressed in Sunday best.

'The only rule,' says the Queenstown paper, quoting the event's website, 'is that people wear a helmet.' The riders, that is. Everyone else wears a hat. I have never seen so many cowboy hats in one place. Of various makes and models, the cowboy hats look somewhat odd perched on men in three-quarter pants

Numbering off.

and bare-shouldered women in slinky short frocks. It's going to a scorcher. The high-country sun has sent temperatures into the mid-twenties by the programmed 11 a.m. start time.

Grant and Ferg, besides being cheeky to each other and to a few guys heckling them from on top of a bright-blue horse float, have some preliminary housekeeping announcements for the crowd.

Sunburn: 'Get a helping of sun block from the St John Ambulance folk — slap it on for a dollar. Good cause, too.'

Toilets: 'Make sure you go early to the Portaloos around the ground. No, it's not a good thing to be visiting them late in the day. Go early.'

When it comes to describing the betting process, the announcer's voice takes on a serious tone: 'We had a tote going here once. It's equalisator betting now, and that's because of the actions of one chap.' He goes on to explain how a Queenstown newspaper reporter assigned to cover the Glenorchy Races a few years ago refused to pay the price of admission, claiming media should be allowed into the ground free of charge. Irked, the reporter filed his story, pointing out there was totalisator operating at the Glenorchy Races (a more serious form of gambling than the equalisator system commonly seen at community horse-racing events). Wellington officialdom in the form of the New Zealand Racing Board and the Department of Internal Affairs got wind of Glenorchy's tote and clamped down on it.

'So, that buggered the totalisator. Now we have the equalisator,' says Grant. Or is it Ferg? I can't tell them apart. 'You can still have fun with it, though. Get your bets on now for the first race on the card, the Walk-Trot-Gallop. Have I got that right, Fergy?'

Every year, the course commentators broadcast the reporter's name and the story behind his unpopular, many would say gratuitous, whistle-blowing. It has become part of the legend of the GY Races. The commentators use portable microphones and wander about the area around the finish line, interviewing visitors lined up at the rail and poking fun at competitors, officials — and the beer-swilling guys from Waikaia on the horse-float grandstand behind them. Their broadcast, spiced with 'bloody', 'bugger', 'bastard' and 'a word rhyming with duck', is an entertaining mixture of respectful comment and ribald side-swiping. It fits with the country casualness of the event not to mention the sportingly fine weather and spectacular surroundings. The Humboldt Mountains — 'Remember them?,' say the commentators, 'They're the Misty

Heading up for the first race, with Mount Nox in the distance.

Mountains of *The Lord of the Rings* trilogy' — are a dramatic if humbling backdrop. Summer heat has reduced their snow cover to patches resembling ancient hieroglyphics, spelling awesome in any language.

No chance of a Head of the Lake 'weather bomb' today. But there's been one before. Everyone remembers the 1994 races.

From late morning the sky began to darken over Mount Earnslaw/ Pikirakatahi until it became as sinister as Mount Doom, the seat of power of Tolkien's tyrannical Lord Sauron. The mountains around Earnslaw began to rumble with thunder. Lightning flashed. It was the kind of electrical storm that causes travellers in these mountains to marvel at the power of nature. In 1948, the London-based *Wide World Magazine* published an artist's impression of Bill O'Leary and Dolly reacting in a startled manner to a bout of thunder and lightning. The caption under the artwork explains why: 'Great boulders brought down by the concussion of the thunder'.

At the 1994 Glenorchy Races, where the first few races had been completed in warm, unnaturally muggy conditions, no one could have imagined what was to come. The rain made an abrupt entrance and was soon belting down at the rate of an inch an hour. Ponds grew on the low patches around the race course and the rugby field in the centre, the parking space. When it looked unlikely the rain would let up in the next couple of hours, the whole event was called off around 2.30 — one of the few times it has been affected by weather since the football club became involved in its organisation.

For a time the storm seemed to be stationary over Glenorchy. Lightning forked through the rain, and thunder rocked the area. Between flash and thunderclap the delay was hardly noticeable. The lightning was right over the town. Ordinarily, thunder takes about three seconds to travel a kilometre following the flash. It was the worst possible time to be trying to load horses into truck and trailer. But it had to be done. Visitors wanted to leave before the road to Queenstown was washed out. Locals wanted to get home pronto. Then there were the television people.

A television documentary crew led by presenter-poet Gary McCormick was in town to make a programme about the Glenorchy Races for Gary's *Heartland* series. They got footage of horses, riders and punters and into the bargain captured the drama of the electrical storm and its flood effects. There was some quick rewriting of the storyboard for the doco because the storm suddenly became a focal point. It caused an almighty flood in the Dart River, which became a 'banker' covering the gravel islands all the way across the braided delta area. The Dart that day hit an estimated 2,200 cubic metres per second. That's an awful lot of water. By comparison, the same river during the November 1999 flood, which pushed Lake Wakatipu to record levels, was only half the volume — a flood flow nonetheless. The 1994 'weather bomb' was a local phenomenon. Lake levels went up but not seriously so.

Weather watchers calculated a rainfall of sixteen inches (forty centimetres) in thirteen hours, which is something you would expect west of the Main Divide but rarely on its eastern flanks. Unused to the intensity of the downpour, hillsides along the Dart River and its tributaries were scarred by rock and tree avalanches. Lake Wakatipu's upper reaches were stained brown by flood sediment and littered with branches and tree trunks.

Jim Veint, one of the event organisers, and his partner, Ros Angelo, made it home safely to Arcadia Station that afternoon, and watched in amazement as the lightning and rain continued into the evening.

Looking back, Jim calls it a one-in-1,000-year storm. A freak event, he reckons: Australian bush fires around that time, which sent a wedge of warm air, ash and brown smoke high into the atmosphere over the Tasman Sea in the direction of southern New Zealand, might have had something to do with it. The rainfall knocked out power to Arcadia and other outlying properties, washed out the Paradise road for a couple of days (the Veints got out by tractor before road repairs were completed), and altered the course of the River Jordan.

It was a miracle no one died in the storm, given the number of people on camping holidays. There were dramas aplenty. A Lilo (inflatable mattress for water recreation) floated out of a tent at the Oxburn/Twelve Mile, carrying a child into the flooded river delta. A helicopter was involved in the rescue. In the Buckler Burn a hut occupied by a family with an eighteen-month-old baby started to move off its foundations, causing the family to flee in the middle of the stormy night.

My first experience of the Glenorchy Races is the 2008 event, and I am to keen catch up with Jim Veint. I find him in front of the equalisator tent writing horses' names and numbers on a whiteboard. He's helped with the running of more than forty of these events. I ask him how the equalisator works.

When the equalisator is closed before the running of each race, the numbers of the competing horses are applied by ballot to letters of the alphabet corresponding to the tickets sold. Instead of placing bets on individual horses — the totalisator method — the punters simply buy lettered tickets at $1 a pop, and listen out for the numbers from ground announcements. A dividend, minus a small commission for the rugby club, is paid out on the winning horse only. It's a system more akin to a raffle than gambling. But make sure you collect your winnings on the day. They'll disappear into the fundraising account otherwise.

'It's taken some of the thrill out of it,' says Jim. 'In the tote days, a policeman would come along from Queenstown and make sure everything was being run properly. We never had a problem.'

The equalisator method has tended to discourage 'surprise' entries, originating mainly from Southland — thoroughbred horses capable of running the hind legs off the local hacks. Yet even if the owners of these 'secret' horses (Jim's name for them) backed them on the tote, they were never likely to make big money. At least, not the kind of money they could make on the regular TAB racing circuit.

Jim has forty-one horses listed so far — well down on the seventy-odd of the tote years — but they are still arriving even with the first race about to start, and the tally could reach fifty. In the early years horses would arrive by barge from various lake stations and in trailers brought over the stony and slip-prone Haast Pass road from the West Coast. The trip over the pass was as much of a challenge as the racing.

'Riders never used to wear helmets in those days,' says Jim. 'As few rules as possible — that was the approach. We still try to keep things simple.'

Jim Veint registering entrants.

And the programme?

'We've kept the same race programme since nineteen sixty-four with the addition of the Ladies' Gallop and Local Gallop.'

Jim was the first secretary and captain of the Lakeside Football Club, and a prime instigator, with Wattie Watson of Routeburn Station, the club's first president, in developing the race meeting out of the tradition of a gymkhana. Both men played rugby and rode horses, and were relatively good at the two pursuits. In a rugby career spanning twenty-eight years Jim played in the backs, practically every position. He played ten games when he was fifty — his last season.

His father, Lloyd, is here today, looking dapper with a necktie. He handed over the running of Arcadia Station to his only son about the time these race days were initiated. He is ninety-four now and living in Queenstown with help at home from daughter Gale. What a life he's had at the Head of the Lake. Scheelite miner, crack-shot deer culler, farmer, guest-house proprietor and, in retirement, artist and fishing guide. At the age of eighty-eight, he guided two American anglers on a fly-fishing expedition to Hollyford and Southland rivers. Until arthritis got to his fingers, he was a dab hand at painting, too. One of his works is of Bill O'Leary (whom Lloyd met) and packhorse Dolly, with mountain beech forest and tall peaks as a backdrop — the kind of Dart country Lloyd himself revelled in as a hunter. He has attended many a race meeting at Glenorchy.

Funds raised by the Glenorchy Races over more than forty years have given the district an array of new services and mod-con hardware. Chalk up television reception, a swimming pool, a new ambulance, flasher rugby clubrooms, and improved fire-fighting, medical, library and school amenities.

A bugle announces the close of betting for the first race.

The public-address system informs everyone that there has been a bit of a delay. The starter, who has done the job for years, in fact was one of William Gilbert Rees's right-hand men, has 'tested positive for steroids'. Never mind, it is a sedate start to the day's racing. The twenty-two horses in the field set off at a walk as prescribed by the rules of the race, with one doing it sideways, prompting Ferg to tell the crowd it could be Monday before the race is over.

The jokes might be recycled but they still go down well: 'If there's anyone from Jellymeat here today, they might be interested to know the horse going sideways is only one can away!'

The winner of the Walk-Trot-Gallop, sponsored by Routeburn Canyoning, is

A thirsty nag

I n the 1950s, when the annual race day was a community sports day or
gymkhana, the races attracted a down-home bunch of homestead ponies,
station hacks, and hard-bitten miners' horses. Ben Gollop's Nugget was
among them, a chestnut gelding, half draught and ornery. Ben used to ride
Nugget to the scheelite mine in the hills above Glenorchy, and the horse would
be turned out for haymaking work as well in the hay season.

Ben's son, Rory Gollop, would be home on holiday from boarding school at
gymkhana time. He remembers those race days, and one in particular. His
father was riding Nugget and lined up at the far end of the track. The
competitors came thundering down the back straight, turf flying from under
the large feet of the working horses. Instead of rounding the corner, Nugget
bolted out the gate and down the road towards the Mount Earnslaw Hotel (he
had been there before). By the time Ben got Nugget turned and back to the
track the other horses were over the finish line.

… 'Wait for it, I can see one official talking to another official and that other
official is, well, we'll get the result to you some time soon' … Horse K, ridden by
a woman named Jess. The payout is $17.50 — 'That'll buy you a litre of petrol'.

There are ten races to get through by about 5 o'clock Glenorchy time, with
a lunch break of half an hour promised somewhere in the middle of the
programme. Each race is wrapped in a warm fuzz of waggish commentary. The
way the horses get spaced out early — and the distance between first and last in
each race — confirms the tradition of variable fitness and ability among the
entrants. By the look of them and their solid build, many of the horses are more
used to slogging it out on the hills, mustering sheep and driving cattle, than
going flat out round a race track. There appear to be few thoroughbreds, sleek
and high-strung, among them. But, really, I'm no judge of horse flesh.

The event's website carries a line right out of rodeo: 'This is not riding for
the faint hearted'. The blonde rider who crashed from her steed down the back
straight during the relay race and got a crack on her helmeted head from a hoof

Another flood

In November 2002 another 'thunder plump' hit the Head of the Lake, bringing torrential rain to the Dart catchment. In the headwaters of a small creek feeding Diamond Lake, dams formed from fallen branches and trees and when the dams broke, a flash flood ensued, so powerful and loaded with sediment that it raised ground level at the creek's fan, near where it enters the lake, by about a metre. The gravel that came down that day caused the death of about a hectare of lake-side forest. It is close to where Heaven's Gate once was, and Peter's Tomb is still to be found. The site today, just off Paradise Road, is an open parking area for visitors to the lake. It is marked by numerous grey spars of red beech trees, which were fatally debarked by the rush of gravel and rocks brought down in the flood. Something similar might have happened about one hundred years ago. The dead trees in this area are mostly same-age. A new crop of red beech is growing up through the gravel.

as the horse passed over her, would probably agree. For a few minutes she lay on the track on her side facing away from the crowd, knocked out, with one hand trembling. By the time the ambulance arrived, and thanks to prior help from first-aiders, she was able to get up, smile and walk to the vehicle.

For the punters, it's a picnic day out with family and friends, and a chance to wear a cowboy hat. Not to worry if you haven't brought food. Over by the rugby pavilion are food stalls selling savoury fare such as whitebait patties and venison burgers, and dessert in the form of strawberries and cream. The whitebait are a coastal delicacy, of course, but the venison and strawberries are Head of the Lake specialities that appeared on menus at the Paradise and Arcadia guest houses in a past era. The food is a fundraiser for the Glenorchy School. I see Mandy Hasselman among the volunteers behind the tables, and husband Mark is somewhere in the clubrooms preparing the food.

Glenorchy, like many remote towns, has few elderly among its residents. As the Head of the Lake Community Plan notes, the elderly are under-represented

Peter's Tomb.

because later in life they tend to move to areas where there is appropriate health care and support for them. The race day brings back a few of the old faces to visit, Lloyd Veint is an example, but the 2008 crowd is largely young to middle-aged, with families predominant, and many of them have come for the action. They wouldn't miss it for quids.

The saddling race is like something out of the Mel Brooks' comic Western of the 1970s, *Blazing Saddles*. It involves a race in two parts on the home straight — a sprint from the start/finish line, bare back, to the other end of the straight, where the contestants must throw over and secure a saddle then ride back to finish. Speaking from the experience of previous years, the announcers warn the riders to make sure the girth strap is fastened good and tight. Some riders are unseated on the sprint to the finish. The last rider makes it with his backside slewing one way then the other down the home straight, with his predicament summed up by the announcers: 'She's a hard road, boy, finding the perfect mount.'

Blazing saddles under a blazing sun. For much of the day the sun remains searingly high overhead — a UV holocaust for those prone to sunburn.

When lunch time is declared, it's time to streak. The young man running naked along the home straight is not so much out to shock and stun as to fulfil a tradition, it seems. The crowd reacts accordingly, with admiring amusement. He must be the least bothersome streaker of all time. One hand masks private parts and with the other he waves the wave of a stellar performer. Just as suddenly he is gone, and the punters in the crowd are invited back to the equalisator tent to place more bets.

I make a couple of visits to the betting tent, buying half a dozen tickets each time to share with my family. There are winning tickets both times, with payouts of $11 and $7 — a fifty per cent return on investment. I doubt if tote betting would top this.

On my second visit to the betting tent, the busiest place on the ground after the bar tent, two young guys, apparently new to the area and keen trampers, are seeking the advice of one of the ticket sellers about where they should go next. It seems they have already been in the Dart Valley because with German accents, they say they visited a rock shelter at Chinaman's Bluff, where a man was camped.

'A real mountain man,' says one of the trampers enthusiastically. 'Alone but friendly.'

As they make their bets, the fellow dispensing tickets tells them about the great walking to be had in the Caples Valley. Then, before they get swallowed up among the punters, I approach them with a question: 'That man you were talking about at Chinaman's Bluff,' I say. 'What did he look like?'

'Not too big,' says one of the Germans. 'Whiskers.' Then the other cut in: 'What I remember is a blue cap and red hair sticking out.'

'When was this?' I ask.

'Just yesterday.'

'Thanks.'

So the Lark is at Chinaman's Bluff now. Arawata Bill was in his prime in his sixties and the Lark is no different, judging by the way he moves around this country. It's an easy day trip to Chinaman's. A rough road meets the entrance to the trampers' track. Given the recent spell of dry weather, the fords along the road should be okay to negotiate with my townie's car. I'll go tomorrow.

Back in the 1990s I passed a rock shelter at Chinaman's on a trek down the Dart from the Cascade Saddle. But I want to be sure about where I'm going, and ask around for directions. Dick Watson, 'track master' for the day at the corner by the main gate (the new crop of grass seemingly worked a treat), says he has an idea where Arawata used to shelter but will phone his son, Gordon, to make sure. According to Dick, Gordon has often run the tramping tracks in the district to get fit for competitive back-country foot races like the gut-busting Southern Traverse and is bound to know. Like other endurance athletes he can run, in a matter of hours, tracks ordinary people take days to traverse.

Back comes the information — yes, there is a rock biv in the bush, about a hundred metres from the edge of it, at the north end of the bluff area. This is a good enough steer for me. I'll head out in the morning.

Dick, meanwhile, is pleased with GY Races '08. He's heard that about 1,800 people paid admission, a bigger crowd than the past couple of years, making for a bigger fundraising kitty. In this district the Glenorchy Races, tote or not, are a safer bet for community projects than the New Zealand Lottery Grants Board.

Portrait of the South Island kōkako on a fruiting kanono Coprosma grandifolia tree.

PAUL MARTINSON/MUSEUM OF NEW ZEALAND TE PAPA TONGAREWA

CHAPTER 9

A Legendary Land

Knowing less now, and alone,
These things make for me
A gauge to measure the unknown
— Lake, mountain, tree,
  Sings Harry.

From 'Sings Harry', by Denis Glover, 1951

The road to Chinaman's Bluff, which at times, because of flood-deepened fords and axle-deep mud, is not for the faint-hearted tarseal traveller, extends as far north into the Head of the Lake district as a vehicle can go. Landmarks abound: Rees River, Camp Hill, Earnslaw Burn, Diamond Lake, Arcadia, Paradise, Mill Flat, Dan's Paddock.

I pause at Paradise. The Ockwells, who formerly managed the Paradise estate under the direction of the Paradise Trust, have moved to Dunedin, and in their place is another young couple, Per Lindstrand and Rachael Bennett, who are from England. They manage the camping and hut accommodation at Paradise, and earn income from working with the Dart Stables horse-trekking business nearby. Arriving in the Glenorchy area in 2004, they were struck by not only the scenic nature of the Head of the Lake but also by its horsy nature. They are putting a stake in the ground. They've bought a piece of land at Glenorchy and will build a house.

Per meets me as I pull up at the cottage. Swedish-born, he is tall and athletic. His family moved to England when he was three. Paradise House, as run-down and romantically rustic as I remember it, is next to where the Paradise managers live. Per confirms the trust has plans to restore the old home and guest-house of William and Kate Mason. It is over 120 years old now and looks vulnerable to the elements. A peacock strides past, towing its improbable cerulean tail — a flashback to an elegant, imperious age and a decorative motif, perhaps, for a Paradise House restoration project.

I'd asked Per earlier if he could show me a couple of the intriguingly named sites at Paradise: the Garden of Eden, Rock of Ages and Adam's Armchair. He's giving up an hour of his horse-trekking work to show me these things. We climb into his ute and drive through the Middle Earth beech forest to the Garden of Eden, a sun-trap of a glade, open to the north and cuddled by beech forest on three sides. Besides a red-brown weatherboard cottage for visitors, with a north-facing verandah and armchairs, Eden has a smaller Hobbit-like structure, grass-roofed, that serves as a sauna. With personal heating of that sort, Eden is complete.

'This way for Adam's Armchair,' says Per. 'I'm up here every other week — it's our water supply.' He points out a black polythene pipe snaking through crown fern beside the little tinkling stream. Striding ahead, he leads me steadily upwards by way of a rough-hewn track till we get to an ancient red beech tree, long deceased, perhaps toppled by wind. Between the great buttresses of this fallen lord of the forest there is a natural seat, high off the ground. Adam must have had long legs.

'And back here,' says Per, 'that's the Rock of Ages.' He points out a worthy contender for the name, a massive block, the size of a mansion, garnished by mosses, ferns and an occasional epiphytic tree. From Adam's Armchair you could mistake the Rock of Ages for a vegetated cliff or the forest interior extending dimly into the distance.

Per needs to get back to his horses, and I need to get on my way to — here's hoping — a meeting with the Lark. The road continues north along the valley floor to Mill Flat, where pasture for red cattle replaced the red-beech forest a long time ago. Over some decades the forest was converted to weatherboards and posts, sent off by lake steamer to Kingston then by rail into Southland to house farmers and fence their fat lambs. Matai and rimu trees partnering the beech in this forest were turned into elegant flooring and framing timber for southern settlements.

At the top end of Mill Flat a cattle stop marks the end of Arcadia land. It's all conservation land or national park from here. The road runs on now through Dan's Paddock, a showcase for matagouri, and through ford after ford, till, at Chinaman's Flat, apparently once a discrete campsite for early Chinese gold-miners, a shiny new information kiosk announces the beginning of the Rees-Dart track at nearby Chinaman's Bluff. Last chance to use a flush toilet, too. Flush toilet? What would Bill O'Leary and his contemporaries make of that?

Bill gets hero treatment on the information panels. Granny Aitken is also featured, and so, too, the valiant mohua and Operation Ark's battle to protect the nationally endangered forest songbird from furry predators in this area.

It's a powerful place, Chinaman's Bluff. It is tempting to call the mighty cliffs limestone, as there's a resemblance: in fact, they are made of older stuff, rocks going back to a time when the embryonic New Zealand land mass lay beneath the sea floor, and part of it was transforming under intense heat and pressure to become the schist of Otago. The bluff's great southern wall protects campers from raging northerly winds. In January 1988, Ron and Sara Keen from Dunedin were camping here with another couple. Ron, a surveyor, was used to the outdoors and to birdlife. He had spent a lot of time in Mount Aspiring National Park. Around dawn, both couples were awoken by a melodic bird call so powerful it made for lively conversation over breakfast. All agreed the call wasn't from a tūī or a bellbird. They concluded it must have been the voice of a South Island kōkako.

Over the generations, Chinaman's Bluff has gazed down on a passing parade of people of many motivations, including surveyors, explorers, prospectors, mountaineers, campers, trampers, kayakers, rafters, jetboaters, and farmers driving cattle or sheep. Sheep did not fare as well as cattle on the remote, wet flats through the middle reaches of the Dart Valley — Dredge Flat, Daley's Flat, Cattle Flat — and eventually all farm stock was removed as the conservation ethic asserted itself, claiming ecological damage from cattle encroaching into unfenced forest margins.

Till a few years ago four-wheel drive vehicles used to be able to get past Chinaman's Bluff. Then floods in the Dart River cut into the gravelly, grassed

REES VALLEY 13 km
NO EXIT
GLENORCHY 7 km
ROUTEBURN 19 km
PARADISE 13 km
INVINCIBLE 9 km
KINLOCH 19 km

Weave a circle round him thrice
And close your eyes with holy dread
For he on honey-dew hath fed
And drunk the milk of Paradise

'Kubla Khan',
Samuel Taylor Coleridge,
1816

The way to Paradise.

apron of land that once carried the vehicle track, chopping off vehicle access and forcing a new alignment for the walking track. This involved some blasting and a new, curving metal bridge around a rock overhang.

I am looking for a rock shelter about a ten-minute walk north, past where the vehicle wheel tracks are rudely interrupted by a two-metre drop into the river's easternmost braid. At the northern end of these river flats, in the absence of any DOC signpost pointing out a rock shelter, I begin looking for signs of past activity at the forest edge.

The forest here is partly open and dotted with ancient piles of rock debris brought down by the glacier. Bare and blackened patches suggest campsites in the past. I poke about, peering into the interior.

'Hey, Lark! You in there?'

I call again.

This time there is a response. A voice but I still can't see him.

'Come on up! Another hundred yards.'

There is no obvious track. I wonder how the Germans found him. Crunching my way over fallen branches I reach a boulder about the size of a two-storey house, the lower side of which is an overhang large enough to shelter two people, three at a squeeze. This can't be the Lark's lair. It is empty.

'Come around the top side!'

And there he is, a Swanndri-clad figure standing beside a dark gap formed by another gigantic straight-sided schist boulder that has come to rest against the lower rock. At least three storeys high, the one forming the roof is bigger than the Rock of Ages. Both boulders could have split off the cliff, probably thousands of years ago. The result of this clash of two monoliths is a shelter where half a dozen campers could comfortably find a roof over their heads.

'Welcome to Hotel Twilight,' says the Lark. 'It's dusk all day.'

True enough, the forest canopy high overhead together with the sloping roof of rock make the interior of the bivvy a gloomy place,

Siren's song

'Like a siren's song, the call of the South Island kōkako is the most staggeringly beautiful birdsong in the world.'

Rhys Buckingham, after hearing and seeing a kōkako, Glenroy River, Murchison, November 1996.

and it takes me a few moments to discern the layout and its contents. The bivvy is open on two sides and campers in the past have obviously done some landscaping to form flat areas for cooking, conversing and sleeping.

If the Earnslaw Burn's Starlight Hotel is a spacious five-star camp site, this one would struggle to gain three stars. There is no starry mountain view and no water supply closer than the river. For seating, there are two wooden ABC beer crates, labelled with the company stamp: 'Make your empties go another round'. Someone's taken the advice: the bivvy contains no empties. A curious honeycomb pattern, not at all characteristic of schist, decorates the ceiling, suggestive of a bat roost. In a downpour, this place would be a winner, even with native long-tailed bats for company.

'Not a patch on Earnslaw Burn in fine weather,' says the Lark. 'But if you're caught short in a storm, it's as good as gold.'

Out of self-interest I ask about the sandflies, whether they're a problem.

'A few, yeah, before rain. But nowhere near the numbers waiting to ambush visitors at the kiosk and around the carpark. I just say the bar's closed if they're niggling me.'

'Heard about you at the Glenorchy Races yesterday. Did the Germans camp with you?'

The Lark leans towards a little gas burner hissing a billy towards a cup of tea. 'No, I bumped into them down by the big erratic boulder. Boiling up a brew, I was. Grab a seat. It's your turn now.'

The bivvy looks lived in, with the Lark's sleeping bag laid out on an inflatable pad, and other accoutrements of camping strewn about. The first people here might well have come upon the scattered remains of moa, adzebill and other flightless birds, now extinct, that chose this shelter as their last resting place. Perhaps the moa-hunting Waitaha people knew this bivvy, too, stayed overnight and awoke to the kind of dawn chorus that made early European explorers gasp in wonder — a dawn chorus that included the bells of bellbirds, the trumpeted melodies of tūī, and the reverberating bong calls of kōkako. It would be several hundred years before the white men came with astonishingly new technology and a menagerie of weird and wonderful animals.

If only … if only, through some modern magic, the skins and skeletons of South Island kōkako found today in museum collections in New Zealand and overseas — as many as 200 skins — could be brought back to life. The species would have a chance then. Imitating the character of the bird itself, most of the skins are hidden from view — stored away in cool, dark places in museum basements, mute and staring glass-eyed. There are enough South Island kōkako at the American Museum of Natural History in New York to fill the valleys at the Head of Lake Wakatipu — twenty-eight specimens all told. Imagine the music of such a flock cascading through the Dart, Routeburn and Caples forests. Even farther from home than New York are the fourteen skins at Cambridge University Museum and the ten at Liverpool Museum. Eight skins are held at the Australian Museum in Sydney. New Zealand holdings including the Museum of New Zealand Te Papa Tongarewa's twenty-eight mounts and skins, nineteen at Canterbury Museum and thirteen in Otago Museum.

Little more than statistics and curiosities now, and part of a sad record, they represent the feverish, competitive collecting and exporting that went on during the late nineteenth century. Add the birds taken for sport or pot to that toll and you can see why humans should be counted among the main predators of kōkako in the south, together with tree-climbing ship rats and stoats. Possums have also contributed to the slaughter, raiding nests for eggs and chicks (chicks confronted by possums are liable to leap out of the nest to their doom) and competing with the kōkako for forest fruit and young shoots. Habitat loss is not an issue for kōkako. There is ample protected space.

Kōkako are long-lived. They may survive beyond twenty years. Reports of contact with the bird in the last twenty years suggest there are survivors still occupying remote catchments where predators are in low numbers going into the twenty-first century.

How many New Zealand bird species have come back from the dead? Answer: enough to be significant. Certainly enough to encourage South Island kōkako searchers. The best-known example is the takahē, *Porphyrio mantelli hochstetteri*, 'rediscovered' in Fiordland's subalpine Takahe Valley on the national park side of Lake Te Anau. Takahē were found browsing the tussock grassland there in 1948 — exactly fifty years after the previous record of the species.

The takahē's fame as a bird rebounding out of extinction has spread far and wide. Bus-borne Japanese tourists in particular are aware of it and many of them make a beeline for the takahē compound at the Te Anau Wildlife Centre

Trick of the light

anting to see a South Island kōkako close up, I call the Otago Museum's natural sciences curator, Otto Hyink, and make an appointment. Out the back of the museum, in the modern storage area, Otto lines up three birds for me. Two are perching on the same mount. Expecting to see the blue-grey plumage of the birds, I am puzzled by their colour under the fluorescent lighting. All three mounted birds are as brown as coffee beans, with one bird, seemingly younger, a paler form, and its wattles are both smaller and lighter in colour than those of the two other birds. Then I start photographing, using the digital camera's built-in flash and play back the images on the camera's LCD screen. The plumage is not brown but blue-grey, just like most of the photographs and paintings of the bird.

A trick of the light conspiring with the unusual construction of the feathers explains the mystery of so many different descriptions of the South Island kōkako's colour … 'dark', 'very dark', 'almost blackish', 'dark grey', 'dark blue', 'slate grey', 'blue-grey', 'lilac-grey' and so on.

I take several photographs. They come out pretty much the same. I am left thinking that under the fluorescent lights in the windowless storage area the birds appear a different colour compared to what they look like under flash, and perhaps under sunlight. Tūī, too, are chameleons, reflecting a rich shiny black in dim settings, and metallic blue-green in brighter conditions.

Artist Paul Martinson, who illustrated *Extinct Birds of New Zealand* with water-colour portraits, says he has to wrestle with changing light and variations in reflected colour. Colour, he says, is affected by the quality of the light at any one time. Wavelengths vary in different environments. A leaf is not intrinsically green — and South Island kōkako not always lilac-grey.

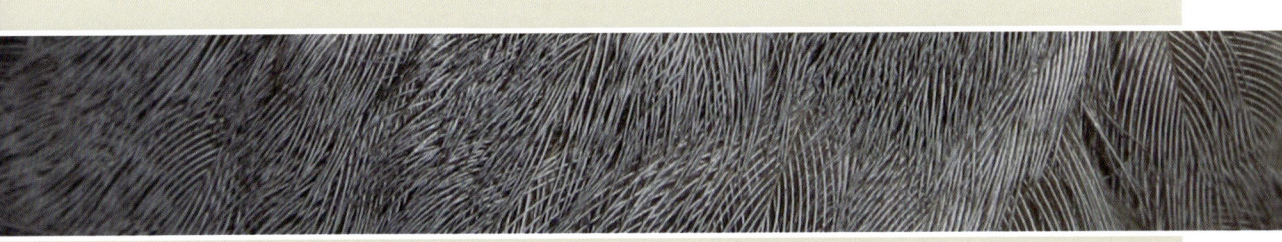

when they pass through the town on the way to or from Milford Sound. There are other examples of 'rediscovery'. In the 1970s, kākāpō, the flightless forest parrot of the night, were found in surprisingly good numbers in a remote southeast corner of Stewart Island, and a long-lost seabird, the magenta petrel of the Chatham Islands, *Pterodroma magentae*, also known as taiko, turned up on the southwest coast of Chatham Island in 1978. These birds were later found in nest burrows under forest. In 2003, another seabird, the New Zealand storm petrel *Pealeornis māoriana*, was 'rediscovered' by seabird enthusiasts in the Hauraki Gulf region one hundred years after the last sighting. Several of these dainty birds were photographed on subsequent trips. One was caught, banded and released.

Despite the rediscoveries, the history of New Zealand bird extinctions has a calamitous look about it. Some forty per cent of the birds unique to the New Zealand ornithological region have become extinct since the first people arrived. Of every ten indigenous species, four have gone forever. American evolutionary biologist and biogeographer Jared Diamond describes New Zealand's extinction history as 'the worst tragedy to befall the world's island biotas'. We have lost a lot.

Are humans entirely to blame? Yes, emphatically. But there is a smaller voice arguing circumstances beyond human control. In the early 1990s I travelled from Dunedin to the Dart Bridge moa-hunter camp site with Otago University archaeologist/anthropologist Atholl Anderson and artist Chris Gaskin. Atholl had studied the site and Chris was reconnoitring it so he could paint a scene from 400 years ago — people preparing food, weaving, interacting — for a new book I was writing about Mount Aspiring National Park. The umu pits were awesome and moving to behold. But what I remember most about that day was something Atholl said as we talked about the large number of moa killed and eaten at this and other moa-hunter settlements and how the hunting impacted on the moa's fate. Atholl has written extensively on moa and excavated numerous moa-bone sites, both natural (notably old swamps) and cultural. He said: 'There are things we don't understand about the process of extinction.' He wasn't denying the moa-hunters' devastating impact. But perhaps there were other factors at work?

Environments change over time. Weather patterns vary. Ice ages come along. Rocks move around, get worn down. Plant life adapts, reinvents itself. The fauna adapts, too, through natural selection. The ancient past saw many more species of animal life than exist today. Extinction happens. It is a natural process. Change is nothing to be scared of. But accelerated change, of the kind predicted for the twenty-first century through global climate change, is another matter altogether, potentially a time of mass extinction.

Moa inhabited New Zealand for a very long time — the only birds in the world to exhibit no trace of wing bones. Long-lived and slow to reproduce, they occupied a wide range of habitats across the country. Their only natural enemy was a giant eagle, also now extinct. Moa were knocked down by a blitzkrieg of hunting within a few generations. But in far-flung parts of the land, including the wilds of Fiordland that probably had never seen people, some moa would have survived. In the end, what killed them off?

Reproductive failure is one notion. Isolated and widely-dispersed species that live a long time but breed slowly are at risk of not achieving rates of replacement. Sometimes the gender balance in the remnant population gets out of kilter (too few females, for example, as has happened to kākāpō). The species declines steadily then dies out. Food supply is another factor. Fire is also implicated. Fires caused by lightning, Polynesian overlanders and nineteenth-century European runholders would have reduced the habitat of some moa species. What else? In his statement about a lack of understanding of extinction processes, Atholl Anderson was also suggesting, I think, that some species become unsuited to their environments. Did the first people to settle New Zealand, bold, efficient and wide-ranging hunters in search of protein, arrive at a time when moa were teetering anyway, and highly vulnerable to hunting?

As for other bird species lost forever, the vast majority have fallen prey to humans and their camp-followers — the introduced mammals that relied as much on scenting prey as seeing and hearing it, a concept alarmingly new to the birds of New Zealand. Rats, cats, dogs, stoats, ferrets, possums, pigs … the list goes on. Then there is the issue of birds introduced to New Zealand from Europe and other regions. Did any of them bring diseases fatal to the local birds? How serious was the competition for food and breeding habitat?

Most extinctions are forever, of course. Christchurch ornithologist Ron Nilsson, who has been chasing reports of South Island kōkako for decades, says he would never expect to come across a bush wren or a laughing owl in his fieldwork. Both these birds became extinct in the twentieth century. South Island kōkako, he says, are a different story. He first searched for them in May 1972, following up a gold miner's report from Boulder Lake, a high and distant corner of the Aorere River catchment in Northwest Nelson. He has been looking ever since, and is not put off by the no-shows.

'These birds are very secretive,' says Ron. 'Herbert Guthrie-Smith [Hawke's Bay pastoralist, author and native bird enthusiast, 1862–1940] organised special expeditions to look for the South Island kōkako on Stewart Island. He was very keen to find and photograph nesting birds. But he failed to see any kōkako, even though they were definitely there in reasonable numbers.'

Ron is critical of plans by the Department of Conservation to transfer North Island kōkako to Secretary Island in Fiordland. 'A mistake,' he says. 'They're a different species.' He is concerned that North Island birds released on Secretary Island might one day interbreed or mix with South Island kōkako, whose identity would then be lost forever.

Fiordland is one of the target areas for him. In 2008, he planned to follow up a hunter's report from the Glaisnock wilderness area, west of Lake Te Anau, of an unusual bird call and a glimpse of a grey bird with rounded wings. He also hoped to go back to Big River in the south of Fiordland. In March 2005, Dunedin geologist Ian Turnbull and a colleague, Duncan Ritchie, reported kōkako-like calls, including powerful 'bong' calls and dueting, in the trackless upper reaches of the valley. There were kākā in the area but no tūī. Calls came in loud and clear in the early morning and evening. Ian knows Fiordland well. He spent five full summers there remapping the geology of southern Fiordland. The Big River bird calls were unlike anything he had heard before.

Six Million Dollar Bird

Pureroa State Forest in the central North Island was the stage for one of New Zealand's most publicised environmental protests in the 1970s, when defenders of North Island kōkako camped in trees to prevent the loss of habitat. In an outburst against the protest, Prime Minister Rob Muldoon described the kōkako as the Six Million Dollar Bird (an estimate of the value of the timber forsaken to save the Pureora population of kōkako).

Ron Nilsson checked out the Big River report twice in 2006, and heard the calls on one of the visits. 'They were mind-boggling,' he says. He counted about thirty separate calls on the first evening, all of them similar and flute-like. Some of the calls comprised five to seven notes. He never caught sight of the source but he was certain the calls were from at least two birds.

In 2007, he investigated an angler's report of a 'big grey bird' at the Nina River south of Lewis Pass. Again, he saw no bird. But he did see fresh kōkako-like moss grubbings, four or five metres square. The grubbings were so fresh he thought the bird might have been close by, watching him. 'I had this eerie feeling.'

And what if Ron — or fellow searcher Rhys Buckingham — comes home one day with conclusive evidence that his long-lost quarry exists? How legendary would that be? What would he do?

Ron doesn't say anything like he'd whoop with delight for a week. No, his response is coolly measured: 'I'd prepare a scientific report for DOC that would trigger an official investigation and hopefully widen the search. Where there's one bird, I reckon there might be two or three of them, keeping within calling range. They're territorial birds, used to keeping in touch.'

Searching of the Nilsson-Buckingham kind, fiercely determined, reflects the hope of a nation: not one species more of New Zealand's unique bird life must be allowed to slip into oblivion. Biodiversity loss must be halted, and the dawn chorus restored to at least something like the old order. Ron Nilsson and Rhys Buckingham simply won't give up.

The lark has a theory about why South Island kōkako are close to the brink of extinction if not beyond it. He believes that their greater use of beech rather than podocarp forest has increased their exposure to predation from exploding stoat populations during beech seeding years.

At the Chinaman's Bluff rock bivvy, perched on wooden beer crates over lunch (remembering Sugarloaf Pass, I brought my own tucker), the Lark and I get down to discussing meatier issues than his mutton sandwiches. He's had kōkako on his mind since our last meeting. He reckons humans in general and New Zealanders in particular are too blasé about the loss of a species.

'You could argue, "What's one more bird? There are dozens left." But it's not a numbers game.' He cradles his enamel mug of tea in both hands and rocks

The Richardson Mountains reflected in a backwater of the Rees River at Glenochy.

back on the beer crate. 'Take a species like South Island kōkako. In looks and in voice, it's a thing of beauty. There's an extraordinary vitality to it that somehow increases the forest's spiritual energy. No question, the forest is sadder without kōkako.'

I relate the story of the Keens and their friends hearing something like a kōkako call around Chinaman's Bluff, and how the call alone — even without a sighting of the bird — remains embedded in their memory twenty years on. Sipping now from the tannin-stained mug, the Lark is contemplative: 'If it's still around in this here neck of the woods it'd be pretty darned lonely. More chance looking round Fiordland or Westland.'

'I know people who are doing just that,' I say. 'Do you get over the Divide yourself much?'

'Nope, plenty of bush and mountains to amuse me here,' says my friend. 'I like being handy to the farming, too. Mountainous places like the country beyond Chinaman's Bluff were impossible to farm so they got turned into national park. Suits me, I can have the wilds and the farms in the same package.'

'What about other services? I mean, don't you ever need a doctor?'

'Hardly. I can sometimes do with a bit of dental treatment, though. Out at Queenstown.'

He goes on to relate a story from his years here on holiday in the 'fifties. It was Easter. A scheelite miner needed to have a tooth extracted. Urgently. With no road to Queenstown, no boat for a couple of days and no small planes flying from the airstrip near Blanket Bay because of bad weather, the miner invited a mate of his to do the extraction. First, the would-be dentist placed the miner's head between his knees, then he took a small wedge of wood and a hammer and whacked the tooth out in one hit.

'Miners were made of tough stuff,' says the Lark.

I am thinking of Bill O'Leary now, of his single-minded grittiness and how he saw the hills and mountains out west being just as capable of producing income and wealth — mineral wealth — as the farms. Arawata Bill spanned two centuries and topped four score years. The Lark is also spanning two centuries but will he live as long? I ask him whether he might ever consider moving to town — in his dotage, so to speak. Dumb question.

In a voice rising contemptuously, he says: 'Me, find a council flat in town or a pensioner cottage?' He shifts nervously on the beer crate and gazes out at the forest interior, where nothing moves and the dank air is bereft of birdsong, perhaps because it's close to the middle of the day and the bush birds are taking a siesta. 'In town, the horizon shrinks. No, I'll be a monkey's uncle before I see the inside of a council flat. The world's overpopulated enough without being reminded of it every day in town. Anyway, where are you headed?'

I tell him about my plans for a book about the Tasman Sea, the ultimate western horizon for a New Zealander.

'You'll be getting in deep there.'

'New territory for sure,' I say. I tell him I'm the kind of writer who serves an apprenticeship with each new project, feeling my way naively with inexperienced eyes. It's as if, as American writer Barry Lopez says, you apply for the position then go on to seek tutoring from people who are always going to know more than you. The trick is to leave behind old perceptions, be open to the tutoring.

'Compared to a region of mountains, valleys, rivers and lakes,' I say, 'the sea is a bit nebulous. For most of us there is no sense of place beyond the breakers, no genius loci.'

'Yeah, but I reckon a sea lion or a selchie would have a sense of place.' His pale-blue eyes narrow and his jaw tenses, exaggerating the ginger stubble. 'Today I bet they'd also see disturbance where they live, much of it caused by humans. Trouble is, humans are far too clever for their own good — too invasive of nature. Isn't it ironic? The more we know about the fabric of nature, the less secure we are. Knowledge is a dangerous thing, as they say. Those things we cannot understand we should let be. Make peace with them. Allow them their mystery.'

Pondering this on my way back from the Chinaman's Bluff rock shelter, I stop to take a picture of the wheel tracks disappearing abruptly into the Dart River. But my new digital camera — a rugged, intelligent, no-nonsense Canon 30D — is jammed. Its LCD screen signals a problem with the two-gigabyte memory card that stores the images, the ones I've taken at the Lark's lair and earlier. Back at Glenorchy and in cell-phone range once more, I contact Jonathan's Camera and Video store in George Street, which sold me the camera. Jonathan himself tells me not to worry; just bring it in when I get back. Images from a corrupted card can usually be recovered.

Next day, I take in the camera with its bung card. The staff are astonished to discover they cannot recover any of the images. The corruption is terminal and highly unusual. They pronounce the camera in good nick and replace the $200 card. The failure of the card is a technical mystery. This is not the kind of mystery of which the Lark speaks. His mysteries apply to nature.

Images of him nag me. He seems to disappear for long periods. Bill O'Leary would do the same from time to time. In May 1929, aged sixty-three, Bill was reported missing in the Upper Arawhata Valley of South Westland, a long way from anywhere. He turned up at Okuru, south of Haast, a couple of months later, no doubt puzzled by the concern for his safety. Poet Denis Glover turned this and other tales of the veteran prospector into a sequence of twenty poems called *Arawata Bill*, which he published five years after Bill died. In the process he helped create a legend. The *Arawata Bill* poems were put to music by Les Cleveland, distributed as a long-play record, broadcast on national radio and in recent times turned into a dramatised DVD, produced by Riverton-based filmmaker Dave Asher and featuring outdoorsman Mike Bennett in the role of the legendary loner.

Denis Glover admitted that he juggled the facts of Bill O'Leary's life to suit his theme of an eccentric mountain rambler facing the elements alone, without fixed abode or worldly possessions beyond those he could pack on a horse. His Arawata Bill craved a simple life in the back of beyond, unencumbered by urban issues and driven by the prospect of a mineral windfall in the next valley or around the next corner.

Wrote Glover in conclusion: 'You should have been told/Only in you was the gold;/Mountain and river paid no fee,/Mountain melting to the river, /River to the sea.'

The Lark is different yet the same, finding fulfilment in the outdoors but not in pursuit of precious metals. He gets his buzz from the landscape, where he is as agile as a falcon and thoroughly tuned in to its natural rhythms, happy as the proverbial lark. As I write this, I can hear the singing strings of English composer Vaughan Williams's landmark *The Lark Ascending*, rising, falling, rising again, a metaphor of optimism and what poet George Meredith, whose work inspired Williams, called 'a silver chain of sound … 'tis love of earth that he instils'.

I meant to ask the Lark back at Chinaman's Bluff whether he ever worried about getting caught up in the middle of a catastrophic earthquake, of the magnitude predicted for the southern New Zealand region in the twenty-first century — in fact, any day now. A Magnitude 8 rupture somewhere along the Alpine Fault would, at the surface, displace the land horizontally by eight to ten metres and vertically by two to four. If the centre of the quake were anywhere near South Westland, where the fault-line's surface trace can be seen from the air angling towards the Fiordland coast, all hell would break loose around the Head of the Lake.

Picture the Lark holed up in a rock bivvy with the mountainsides around him crashing and sliding, and his shelter collapsing, entombing him. Would he worry about meeting such an end, this man of the land? I doubt it.

Swamp forest, Glenorchy Lagoons.

South Island Kōkako

Callaeas cinerea

Orange-wattled crow, organ-bird, gillbird, kōka

The South Island kōkako belongs to a unique avian family — the New Zealand wattle birds, formally called Callaeatidae. Its cousins are the huia, a North Island species that became extinct around 1907, and the North Island and South Island saddlebacks.

In a taxonomic review in 2001, paleoecologists Richard Holdaway and Trevor Worthy identified the South Island kōkako as *Callaeas cinerea*, a species separate from its North Island relative and known in some southern areas in pre-European times as kōka. *Callaeas* is a generic Greek word for cock's wattles, and *cinerea* means ash-grey. The bird was described scientifically from a specimen collected in Queen Charlotte Sound by Captain James Cook's 1777 expedition, decades before the North Island bird was formally described and named.

In the late nineteenth century, the two kōkako were described by Sir Walter Buller in his landmark book on New Zealand's birds as separate species. Later they were deemed to be more closely related and formally described as subspecies.

They continue to be distinguished mainly by the colour of their wattles: lapis-lazuli blue for the North Island bird, deep orange for the South Islander. Researchers are now less certain, however, that wattle colours are separated by Cook Strait. Touches of orange appear in North Island birds, and blue is known to appear with the orange wattles of the South Island species (the orange wattles commonly have a blue base or spots). Perhaps wattle colouring changes with age. The wattles swell in the breeding season and the sexes are difficult to tell apart.

In January 2007, the Department of Conservation in Wellington proclaimed the species extinct when it published a triennial review of the status of New Zealand native fauna and flora — the *New Zealand Threat Classification System Lists 2005*. With this review New Zealand's unenviable list of extinct species increased by seven — six invertebrate animals (three snails, two beetles and a weevil) and the South Island kōkako, 'for which there have been no confirmed sightings for 45 years'. This, said the report, was 'despite searching'. Thus the South Island kōkako became the sixteenth bird to be declared extinct since 1840.

Support for the Department's position came from the Ornithological Society of New Zealand's *Atlas of Bird Distribution in New Zealand 1999–2004*, published in 2007.

The atlas is silent on South Island kōkako, declaring there were no records for the focus years of the survey.

In pre-human times, the species was widely distributed across the South Island and Stewart Island. Sightings ranged from seashore forest edges to high-altitude forest.

The entire western side of the South Island from Northwest Nelson to Fiordland was a stronghold for the kōkako but it was also found in patches of southeast coastal forest, from Dunedin to the Catlins. The Mount Cargill forest overlooking Otago Harbour had 'very plentiful' numbers, according to Otago geologist James Hector. There were reports also from Banks Peninsula.

In the South Island, the kōkako was still fairly common in the 1870s. But from then, it began disappearing at a rapid rate.

Why did no one take the initiative twenty to fifty years ago, when the species was obviously struggling to survive, to intensely search for and protect South Island kōkako? Future ornithologists may well ask that question. Possible answers: perhaps the existence, even if threatened, of the similar North Island kōkako detracted from any action being taken back then. Perhaps the mission looked altogether too hard and laborious. Perhaps officialdom thought it was
a lost cause.

Meanwhile, the reports still come in of presumed kōkako calls and observations, from Fiordland, the West Coast and the Murchison area, and the searching continues. It will not be stilled by the label of extinction applied by the Department of Conservation in 2007.

Doomed? Maybe. Extinct? Not yet.

The Day the Lake Came to Town

In mid-November 1999, I was heading to the Head of the Lake with my wife, Mary, for a tramp in the Caples Valley. The Caples is one of the main valleys on the remote northwestern side of Lake Wakatipu. You loop around Queenstown, Glenorchy and Kinloch to get there. It is always an expedition, never a day trip. You go for the tramping, fly-fishing or bird-watching. In the late 1990s, developers with an eye on short-cutting the Queenstown-Milford Sound experience proposed a gondola development linking the upper reaches of the valley to the Milford highway in the Hollyford, across the Main Divide. At the news of the proposal, 'Gondola Be Gone' bumper stickers blossomed all over southern New Zealand.

We got as far as Queenstown on that trip. It was raining — heavy, unrelenting rain. We checked into the Gardens Parkroyal Hotel near the lake shore in Queenstown Bay. I requested a room with a view over the lake, hopeful of a scenic sunrise. That evening we ate at a restaurant on the Steamer Wharf, where lake water was lapping the deck timbers. The atmosphere inside the restaurant equated to that of a sinking ship. At the entrance, as if to reinforce the analogy, was a showpiece rowboat sitting up on its stern.

Through the night, curious gurgling sounds emanated from the bathroom. They took on a progressively higher pitch as the night wore on. In the morning I looked out towards the lake to see a man making his way slowly towards the historic 1911 Coronation Bath House, now a café, on the gravel foreshore. He was moving slowly because he was wading through water waist-deep and curry-brown from the deluge flowing past the hotel. Horne Creek, normally a bubbling brook, had become an enraged torrent. We decided to sit tight. At 11.45 a.m., a hotel porter arrived at the door, warning us not to flush the toilet. Ten minutes later, we were ordered to evacuate. Lake and creek water were threatening the hotel entrance.

This flood was huge. Queenstown was cut off by landslips, the airport closed. There was no chance of getting to Glenorchy let alone Kinloch and the Greenstone-Caples carpark. The following day the *Otago Daily Times* reported a flood exceeding the level of the infamous 1878 flood. Kayakers were paddling around the lower part of Queenstown's retail area, and I saw a 'No Parking' sign still attached to its white pole floating out of Queenstown Bay, the jetties under water, bench seats in St Omer Park half submerged and the park's weeping willows having plenty to cry about, with their lowest branches well immersed in lake water.

At Glenorchy, about fifteen homes were flooded, and the road link with Queenstown looked as if it had been bombed, with the tarseal ruptured and overturned from numerous washouts. It would be ten days before the road reopened. Boats from Dart Jet and Queens-town launch companies ran a freight and passenger shuttle to and from Queenstown.

Things went exceedingly quiet in the Caples and Greenstone Valleys. The road down that side of the lake was closed for nigh on three months.

Further Reading

Books

Bradshaw, Julia, *Miners in the Clouds: A Hundred Years of Scheelite Mining at Glenorchy* (Arrowtown: Lakes District Museum, 1997)

Dougherty, Ian, *Arawata Bill: The Story of Legendary Gold Prospector William James O'Leary*, new edn (Auckland: Exisle, 2000)

Duncan, Alfred H, *The Wakatipians* (1888), (Arrowtown: Lakes District Centennial Museum, repr. 1969)

Gaze, Peter, *Rare and Endangered New Zealand Birds: Conservation and Management*, (Christchurch: Canterbury University Press, 1994)

Hay, J. R., H.A. Best and R.G. Powlesland, *Kokako* (Dunedin: John McIndoe/ New Zealand Wildlife Service, 1985)

Heather, Barrie and Hugh Robertson, *Field Guide to the Birds of New Zealand* (Auckland: Penguin Books, 1996)

Glover, Denis, *Arawata Bill: A Sequence of Poems* (Christchurch: Pegasus Press, 1953)

Glover, Denis, *Sings Harry and Other Poems* (Christchurch: Caxton Press, 1957)

Griffiths, G.J., *King Wakatip* (Dunedin: John McIndoe, 1971)

King, Carolyn M., *The Handbook of New Zealand Mammals* (Auckland: Oxford University Press, 1990)

Molloy, Les and Craig Potton, *New Zealand's Wilderness Heritage* (Nelson: Craig Potton Publishing, 2007)

Oliver, W.R.B., *New Zealand Birds* (Wellington: A.H. and A.W. Reed, 1930)

Orbell, Margaret, *Birds of Aotearoa: A Natural and Cultural History* (Auckland: Reed, 2003)

Peat, Neville, *Land Aspiring: The Story of Mount Aspiring National Park* (Nelson: Craig Potton Publishing, 1994)

Peat, Neville and Brian Patrick, *Wild Central: Discovering the Natural History of Central Otago* (Dunedin: University of Otago Press, 1999)

Quammen David, *The Song of the Dodo* (New York: Simon & Schuster, 1996)

Schama, Simon, *Landscape and Memory* (London: Fontana/HarperCollins, London, 1995)

Stacpoole, John, *William Mason: The First New Zealand Architect* (Auckland: Auckland University Press/Oxford University Press, 1971)

Tennyson, Alan and Paul Martinson *Extinct Birds of New Zealand* (Wellington: Te Papa Press, 2006)

Turbott, E.G., ed., *Buller's Birds of New Zealand* (Christchurch: Whitcombe & Tombs, 1967)

Reports

Anderson, Atholl and Neville Ritchie 'Pavements, Pounamu and Ti: The Dart Bridge Site in Western Otago, New Zealand', *New Zealand Journal of Archaeology* 8 (1986)

Blakely Wallace Associates, *Glenorchy-Head of the Lake Community Plan* (Glenorchy: Glenorchy Community Association, 2001)

Buckingham, Rhys, *Confirmed Presence of Kokako on Stewart Island* (Invercargill: Department of Conservation, 1987)

Chandler, Peter, *Land of the Mountain and the Flood: A Contribution to the History of Runs and Runholders of the Wakatipu District* (Queenstown: Queenstown and District Historical Society, 1996)

Heath, Sue, *Rock Wrens in the Southern Alps of New Zealand* (Melbourne: Flora and Fauna of Alpine Australasia, CSIRO,1986)

Hitchmough, Rod, Leigh Bull and Pam Cromarty, *New Zealand Threat Classification System Lists 2005* (Wellington: Department of Conservation, 2007).

Holdaway, Richard N., Trevor H. Worthy, and Alan J.D. Tennyson, 'A Working List of Breeding Bird Species of the New Zealand Region at First Human Contact', *New Zealand Journal of Zoology* 28 (2001) 119-187

McFarlane, David, 'A Tourist Paradise: The Development of Tourism at the Head of Lake Wakatipu 1860–1914' (unpublished History honours thesis, University of Otago,1983)

Mulcock C.M., *Tussock Grasslands, South Island, New Zealand: Our Heritage* (Timaru: South Island High Country Committee of Federated Farmers, 2001)

Ockwell, Geoff, 'Understanding Place: A Case Study' (unpublished Physical Education Master's thesis, University of Otago, 2001)

Robertson, C.J.R. et al, *Atlas of Bird Distribution in New Zealand 1999–2004*, (Wellington: Ornithological Society of New Zealand, 2007)

Ross, Malcolm, 'The Ascent of Mount Earnslaw', *The New Zealand Alpine Journal* 1 (1892)

Ross, Malcolm, ed., 'Two Ascents of Mount Earnslaw', *The New Zealand Alpine Journal* 1 (1893)

Scott, Iris (compiler), *The Head of the Lake: A Community Centred on Glenorchy*, (Glenorchy: Runholders/Rees Valley Station,1989)

Turnbull I.M. (compiler), *Geology of the Wakatipu Area* (Lower Hutt: Institute of Geological and Nuclear Sciences, 2000)

Websites

www. glenorchy-nz.co.nz

www.mountainlandrovers.co.nz

www.nevillepeatsnewzealand.com

Index of names

(italicised numbers refer to an illustration)

Acknowledgements

I could not have presented this story without the cooperation of a cross-section of the Head of the Lake community. I am grateful for the generous assistance of runholders Iris Scott and her daughter Kate (Rees Valley Station), Mark and Amanda Hasselman (Temple Peak Station), Jim Veint and Ros Angelo (Arcadia Station) and Geoffrey Thomson (Mount Earnslaw Station). The Paradise Trust's Rory Gollop, Geoff and Grace Ockwell, Per Lindstrand and Rachael Bennett gave freely of their time, knowledge and anecdotes. I delved into the Head of the Lake's early history with the help of Elfin McDonald, Lindsay Kennett, Richard Kennett, Rory Gollop, Pat Gollop, Dick Watson, David Sharpe, David Galloway, Peter Johnson, David McFarlane, Jim Veint and Geoffrey Thomson. Karen Swaine of the Lakes District Museum in Arrowtown provided historical material, and Matapura Ellison and Edward Ellison advised me about the Māori experience of the district. Gerald Arthur of the New Zealand Geographic Board provided information on mountain names and the origin of the names. Linda Holloway gave me information on the Holloway mountaineering legacy, and shearers Ronny Hill and Jim Bool updated me on the practice and history of blade shearing. Thor Davis and David Sharpe shared their possuming knowledge. Dermatologist David W. Young investigated 'birch itch'. I thank them all.

For information about the South Island kōkako and records of it, I am indebted to Rhys Buckingham and Ron Nilsson, whose dedication to the search for the bird is inspiring. John Kendrick, an equally impressive ornithologist and recorder of bird vocalisations, kindly sent me a tape of 'presumed' South Island kōkako calls. I also thank Cagan Sekercioglu, now a bird extinction specialist from Stanford University, California, who reported seeing a kōkako on the Routeburn Track in 1995, and Barry Lawrence, who shared his knowledge of local natural history and the South Island robins. Others who gave me advice on native birds and nature conservation were John Darby, Ian Flux, Sue Heath, Otto Hyink, Ron Keen, Euan Kennedy, Richard Kennett, Les Molloy, Neill Simpson, Philip Temple and Ian Turnbull. Jane Forsyth assisted with Dart Valley geological information.

On the illustrative side, I thank the Lakes District Museum and archivist Karen Swaine in particular, the Hocken Library, Alexander Turnbull Library, Museum of New Zealand Te Papa Tongarewa, Auckland Art Gallery and Department of Conservation for the use of historic photographs and artwork. Thanks also to Allan Kynaston for the map on p. 8. The poetry of Denis Glover is reproduced with the kind permission of the Denis Glover Estate and Pia Glover.

To the team at Longacre Press, especially publisher Barbara Larson and editor Emma Neale, thanks so much for your expertise and support. Creative New Zealand provided a project grant to assist research a few years ago, and I completed the writing with the support of the Creative New Zealand Michael King Writers' Fellowship 2007.

Neville Peat
Broad Bay, February 2008